What Are the Dead Sea Scrolls

and Why Do They Matter?

What Are the Dead Sea Scrolls and Why Do They Matter?

Dr. David Noel Freedman

Dead Sea Scrolls Scholar for Over 50 Years

and Dr. Pam Fox Kuhlken

WILLIAM B. EERDMANS PUBLISHING COMPANY

GRAND RAPIDS, MICHIGAN / CAMBRIDGE, U.K.

Published 2007 by
Wm. B. Eerdmans Publishing Co.
2140 Oak Industrial Drive N.E., Grand Rapids, Michigan 49505 /
P.O. Box 163, Cambridge CB3 9PU U.K.

Printed in the United States of America

11 10 09 08   7 6 5 4 3

Library of Congress Cataloging-in-Publication Data

Freedman, David Noel, 1922-
What are the Dead Sea scrolls and why do they matter? : the straight story from
an expert to you / David Noel Freedman and Pam Fox Kuhlken.
p.   cm.
Includes bibliographical references.
ISBN 978-0-8028-4424-8 (pbk. : alk. paper)
1. Dead Sea scrolls. 2. Qumran community.
I. Kuhlken, Pam Fox.   II. Title.
BM487.F67   2007
296.1'55 — dc22
2007003416

www.eerdmans.com

Contents

Foreword

For my entire adult life I've admired David Noel Freedman and his scholarship, so it is a deep pleasure to recommend his latest work. And consistent with his *modus operandi* over his entire career, Noel has brought in a new, young scholar as his collaborator, in this case Pam Fox Kuhlken.

When it comes to the Dead Sea Scrolls, Noel was there at the beginning. In March 1948, John Trever sent the first photos of the St. Mark's Isaiah Scroll to Prof. W. F. Albright at The Johns Hopkins University in Baltimore. Noel and Frank Cross were the first two students to whom he chose to show the photos. Fifty-eight years later, Noel is still going strong, as evidenced by this latest contribution to the field.

From the 1955 publication of Millar Burrows's book on the Dead Sea Scrolls until now, there has been no shortage of publications about the Scrolls, especially during the past 15 years. There are many good books already, but this book will move to the front of the line, if only because it is aimed directly at a popular audience. Thus, it is simple, clear, and comprehensible; and because Noel had a hand in it, there is delightful humor throughout.

Over the years I've been associated with the Dead Sea

Scrolls Foundation and the publication of the Scrolls, I've often thought that public interest in the Scrolls had reached its zenith, that the flame had been fanned as high as possible. But I've always been wrong. More people are interested in the Scrolls in more places for more reasons now than at any previous time since their discovery. In the face of this ever-increasing thirst for information, *What Are the Dead Sea Scrolls and Why Do They Matter?* will fill the general public's need for distilled and synthesized facts, presented not for scholars, but for the average person. For this reason, it performs an important public service.

This is a mature book, written out of a lifetime of experience in the field of biblical studies by a mature scholar who has a rare gift for communicating with the general public as well as with his scholarly colleagues, along with a scholar who is part of the younger, contemporary generation.

It will be a delight for readers, who are warned, however, that they might not be able to put it down!

JERUSALEM   WESTON W. FIELDS, TH.D., PH.D.
September 15, 2006   *The Dead Sea Scrolls Foundation*

Introducing the Dead Sea Scrolls

When it comes to the Dead Sea Scrolls, we have general questions: *What are they about? Who wrote them, why, and in what language? What's the big deal?*

And paranoid ones: *Was Qumrân another Heaven's Gate or Waco? When do the Scrolls say the world will end? Who's hiding fragments of the Scrolls? How soon before the Scrolls disintegrate?*

Even cynical ones: *How much would a fragment of the Scrolls sell for on eBay? Was there a conspiracy to keep the Scrolls from the public? Sure, theology is fine, but where's the buried treasure? Isn't every Bible just another fragment?*

From sacred meals to celibate hermits, from Roman legions to a Lion of Wrath, Dr. David Noel Freedman, the internationally-renowned expert on the Hebrew Bible and Endowed Chair of Hebrew Biblical Studies at the University of California, San Diego, has thought deeply about all these topics. After studying the Scrolls for over 50 years and publishing over 340 books in the field, Professor Freedman says, "I think I know a little something and I'd like to pass it along to the public, even to all those people not fortunate enough to enroll in my seminars!"

Most of us don't plan on becoming fluent in Hebrew or joining an archaeological dig in Israel. And we don't have the time or means to return to school. At last, here is a book written for everyone who has basic questions about the Dead Sea Scrolls and wants to buff up on the most recently discovered "Wonder of the World." No prior knowledge required. This user-friendly guide with a sense of humor doesn't resort to the jargon found in books written by scholars for scholars.

Dr. Freedman has heard your questions, and has the answers, complete with behind-the-scenes and between-the-lines secrets that only someone on the front lines would know. Here at your fingertips is an introduction to what has been called the greatest archaeological discovery of the twentieth century.

Pam Fox Kuhlken, Ph.D., has graduate degrees in comparative literature, theology, and poetry. After studying at the Hebrew University in Jerusalem, swimming in the Dead Sea and taking mud baths on its shores, and exploring the caves at Qumrân, she still didn't know a lot about the Dead Sea Scrolls, so she asked the smartest guy she knew to fill her in.

With manuscript in hand, she consulted Brian Kelly, one of the sharpest scholars in the business who had studied Hebrew with the man himself, and he offered pivotal remarks and tidied up the final draft. Finally, the finishing touches from Allen Myers and Andrew Hoogheem at Eerdmans improved the book so it was more reflective of the order and symmetry so dear to the Essenes' hearts.

What's All the Fuss About?

It's hard to know where to begin, so let me first ask: What don't we know about the Dead Sea Scrolls?

That's a good question, because we don't really know what we don't know yet. There are many lines in the Dead Sea Scrolls that we can't read very well. Most of the manuscripts are fragments, and each piece requires hours of study before it can be identified and placed in a column of a manuscript. The edges of fragments have been eaten by moisture, fungi, and generations of worms, so nothing fits together clearly. In many ways, the Scrolls are the ultimate jigsaw puzzle.

A lot is missing, but on the other hand, a lot is there. We should probably emphasize what we do know and what we've learned over the last sixty years since their discovery in 1947.

I'd love to have film footage of the Essenes, the religious community who created the Scrolls, as they joined together for meals, prayer, study, deliberation, and work — but that will never happen, of course. And I'd like to know how close they came to living in pure love. The first line of their rule book gives their aim: "To seek God with all one's heart and all one's soul, to do what is good and right before him, as he commanded through Moses and all his servants the prophets, to love all that he has chosen and to hate all that he has rejected." It would be wonderful to know to what extent this really happened at Qumrân.

What Are the Scrolls?

The Dead Sea Scrolls are fragments of papyrus, leather (sheep or goatskin), and, in one case, copper that were once part of complete books in scroll form. They were originally the property of the Essenes, a Jewish sect who made their home in the caves at Qumrân near the Dead Sea. Over 100,000 fragments can be pieced together into over 900 separate documents, with multiple copies of most books, as one would expect of a library. These fragments provide extensive excerpts from the 39 books of the Hebrew Bible (or, as most Christians call it, the Old Testament). There are also fragments from the so-called Apocryphal or Deuterocanonical works (that is, a selection of books accepted as part of the Bible by Roman Catholic and Orthodox Christians, but not by Jews and most Protestants).

When scholars refer to the "Dead Sea Scrolls," however, they usually mean certain non-biblical, sectarian documents such as the Manual of Discipline or the Damascus Document. (More on these documents later.)

The oldest Scroll fragments date back to the third century B.C., placing us within 100 or 200 years of the original composition of books like Ecclesiastes or Daniel. Until the discovery of the Scrolls, the oldest copy we had of the Hebrew Bible dated from the ninth century A.D., about 1,000 years later than the Scrolls! Thus the Dead Sea Scrolls bring us much closer to the times when the Bible was actually written.

Unrolling brittle or decomposing scrolls is a slow and painstaking process. In order to open the Genesis Apocryphon scroll (an Aramaic paraphrase of the patriarchal narratives in Genesis), scholars had to unwind nine layers of interweaving leather.
(The Shrine of the Book, Israel Museum)

Why are the Dead Sea Scrolls important to the general public?

The Dead Sea Scrolls are "the greatest manuscript discovery of modern times," proclaimed Professor William Foxwell Albright (1891-1971), the famous Scrolls expert at The Johns Hopkins University, who was among the first to be told about their discovery. The discovery in itself makes the Scrolls a vital matter for everyone.

More specifically, the Scrolls matter to those of us who are concerned with the Hebrew Bible — those of us who are in any way connected to the religions of Judaism, Christianity, and Islam. The Dead Sea Scrolls link us to the ancient Middle East during a formative period of Judaism and Christianity. Some "sectarian" Scrolls reveal a distinct form of Judaism that didn't survive the Second Temple's destruction by the Roman army in A.D. 70. These Scrolls represent a fascinating transition between the ancient religion of the Bible and Rabbinic Judaism as we know it today, as well as from Judaism to Christianity, the faith that would become the world's largest. Both of these faith traditions, in turn, influence Islam.

Did the Dead Sea Scrolls change the course of biblical scholarship?

They changed the course of biblical scholarship in that they prove that the text of the Hebrew Bible that has come down to us is more reliable than previously thought — that fewer scribal or editorial changes or errors had occurred over the centuries than scholars once imagined. They confirm that by 100 B.C., the canon and the text of authoritative books of the Hebrew Bible had been fixed. Despite some small variations, the Dead Sea Scrolls reflect the same selection of books and have very much the same wording as our current Hebrew Bible.

By the way, it's easy for us to tell which books the Essenes considered to be authoritative. The Dead Sea Scrolls make a clear distinction between the books that were canonical (accepted as definitive) and those that were marginal (because they added certain particulars or otherwise strayed from the community's commonly held beliefs). The peripheral works in the Dead Sea Scrolls had a different format from the canonical ones.

Take a look at the books on your library shelf at home. You'll see that most of them, regardless of their content, have more or less the same height to width ratio: 2 to 1. At Qumrân, only the canonical books had those proportions. (Of course, the Essenes at Qumrân did not yet have bound books, called "codices," as we know them.) What I am referring to is the dimensions of a single column of text written on a scroll. The other, more marginal books have different ratios for their columns.

Does that ratio of two to one have any deeper significance?

It comes from the prophet Zechariah, who describes a vision of a flying scroll (Zech. 5:1-2). Two dimensions of the scroll are given: 20 cubits by 10 cubits, height to width. When people read that, they think it refers to the size of the entire scroll. But what the measurements really define is a single column of text that is exposed when the scroll is unrolled. In a typical scroll, a column such as we ordinary mortals read is about 9 inches by 4½ inches, or, in biblical terms, about half a cubit by a quarter cubit. Thus, in Zechariah's vision the column of text is forty times the normal size! Who reads this giant heavenly scroll, the Torah in heaven? God. And the proportion of his holy text's columns is 2 to 1, height to width. The Essenes used this divine ratio for the canonical books of the Bible.

What languages are the Scrolls written in?

Most are in Hebrew, though we do not know whether the Qumrânites actually spoke Hebrew among themselves or whether they, like almost everyone else in Judea at the time, spoke Aramaic. As the main language of the Bible, however, Hebrew was considered holy and therefore appropriate for religious subjects such as preoccupied the Essenes.

The script that they used to write Hebrew was the so-called Aramaic script, a script with square letters that was very similar to those used in Phoenicia and Greece during that same period. However, occasionally the Qumrânites used another, more ancient script known as paleo-Hebrew. With one interesting exception, they used this script exclusively for the personal name of God (יהוה, YHWH, also known as the Tetragrammaton or "Four Letters"). They did this because they thought that paleo-Hebrew was the script that Moses himself had used.

The exception is the so-called Leviticus Scroll, in which not just God's personal name, but every last word is written in paleo-Hebrew. Since paleo-Hebrew was the Essenes' holiest script, you can imagine how important they thought the various ritual laws were that are contained in the book of Leviticus! Ritual was so important to them, in fact, that they couldn't let the Bible have the last word, but instead they composed their own, stricter version of ritual law, which is contained in the Temple Scroll.

A few Scrolls are written in Aramaic, a language that also appears in parts of Daniel and Ezra in the canonical Bible. The Genesis Apocryphon is the major work among the Dead Sea Scrolls in Aramaic, and we only have a fragment of it. Greek is used only for some place names, and Latin hasn't turned up at all.

If people can't read Hebrew, can they still appreciate a Dead Sea Scrolls museum exhibit or published facsimile?

Absolutely. Very few people, actually, are able to read them, but nevertheless, the Scrolls are impressive to view. Ordinary people can still appreciate them as ancient artifacts regardless of whether they can read them. Fortunately, there are people who can read them, and translations of practically all of the Scrolls are now available, with commentaries and explanations. We can enjoy a film in a foreign language, as long as we read the subtitles. The same resource is available for the Scrolls: the experts provide the translations.

As with other ancient documents you may have seen in a museum, it's helpful but by no means required to be able to read ancient inscriptions. It's enough to enjoy their artistry and mystique, surviving millennia to be seen at last.

Was there a conspiracy to keep the Scrolls from the public?

I wouldn't make charges of a conspiracy. Facsimile editions (that is, exact copies) and photographs of the Scrolls are now widely available for anyone who wishes to study them. And even before they were widely available, practically any scholar who wanted access to the Dead Sea Scrolls could get it, if certain rules were followed. If any charge of conspiracy were to be made, it would be against those who hoard Scroll fragments as a talisman, artifact, or novelty — or as an investment that will later be sold.

However, if there hasn't been a conspiracy, I would say there has been some secrecy. Not long after the Scrolls were discovered, an international editorial team was organized by three parties: the Palestine Archaeological Museum; G. Lankester Harding of the British School; and Père Roland de Vaux of the École Biblique et Archéologique Française in Jerusalem.

Harding and de Vaux, in turn, invited seven other scholars to join them.

Most of these were Protestant Christian and Roman Catholic scholars; no Jewish scholars were included. Such an omission seems strange to us today. Some people claimed Jewish scholars were excluded from the team, accusing de Vaux of being anti-Semitic, but in fact the political situation after the first Arab-Israeli War of 1948-49 made it impossible to appoint Jews to the research team. Jews were allowed in West Jerusalem, but the Scrolls were in the Palestine Archaeological Museum in East Jerusalem, which was in Jordan's hands.

In any event, the international editorial team assigned each Scroll to a different scholar, and each scholar worked at his own pace to publish a critical edition of that Scroll, complete with notes, analyses, and other scholarly details. Some of these scholars produced quickly, some were much slower, and a few never did complete their assignment!

Would there have been a better way to go about publishing the Scrolls? I think so. The Scroll containing the book of Isaiah was published almost immediately because Millar Burrows (1889-1980), professor of biblical theology at Yale, made the best decision of all. Instead of hoarding the manuscripts, documenting them, and performing scholarly analysis behind the scenes, he published a facsimile edition immediately and made the Isaiah Scroll available so that everybody would have equal access to it for their research.

My attitude then and now is that secrecy is bad — it slows things down. I prefer rapid progress. This conforms to my sentiments about the discovery of new documents as well. They should be photographed and made available to one and all.

When did the actual Scrolls become available for public viewing in the United States?

The Scrolls became available to the public in 1991. At that time, the Huntington Library in San Marino, California, had the most extensive collection of photographs of the Scrolls that wasn't directly controlled by the official Scroll editors. (When I refer to "photographs" of the Scrolls, I mean detailed, high-quality images suitable for study, not snapshots such as you might take at an exhibit.) I encouraged William Moffett, the Library Director, to let people see those photographs. Moffett assigned me the task of separating the photographic materials into those that had already been published and made readily available from those which hadn't been seen to date. After being organized, the pictures were released from storage and opened to the public. Additionally, the Huntington provided microfilm copies of the Scrolls to over 80 other libraries, effectively putting an end to limitations on access to them.

What do scholars consider to be the major contribution of the Dead Sea Scrolls to biblical scholarship?

One of the major results of the study of the Dead Sea Scrolls is a much greater recognition of the value of the Septuagint — an important Greek translation of the Hebrew Bible. In many places, the Septuagint differs from the standard Hebrew text, known as the Masoretic Text, which was compiled between the third and tenth centuries A.D. by a group of Jewish scholars known as the Masoretes. Our oldest complete manuscripts of the Masoretic Text date to about the tenth century A.D.

The Septuagint was initiated in the third century B.C., contemporary with the Dead Sea Scrolls. We've always known that the Septuagint is the oldest and most important translation of the Hebrew Bible. Yet scholars have debated over the years as to how reliable the Greek text is, with verdicts ranging from "it's a *paraphrase* of the same text on which the Masoretic is based" (and therefore not as reliable, relatively speaking) to "it's a *faithful* rendering of a *different* Hebrew text" (and so very important). That "different" Hebrew text, hypothetical for so many years, has now been found in the Dead Sea Scrolls.

We can finally say, in other words, that the Septuagint is a *literal* translation of an *actual* Hebrew text that *differs* in certain ways from the Masoretic text. This reestablishes the Septuagint's value as a witness to the Hebrew Bible at an early stage in its transmission.

When scholars are working with translations, they can reconstruct an original, untranslated text simply by translating back from what they have into what they know the original language to have been. They use the German term *Vorlage* ("prototype") to refer to this original text. Scholars working on the Dead Sea Scrolls have found that documents such as 4QSamuel[a] and 4QSamuel[b] (these strange titles refer to copy "a" and copy "b" of the book of Samuel found in Qumrân Cave 4) are much closer to the Hebrew *Vorlage* of the Septuagint than they are to the standard Masoretic Hebrew text. Thus the Scrolls reveal that the Septuagint represents a fairly faithful rendering of a Hebrew text of the Bible that really existed. In other words, it's a good translation. We can trust it.

Since the Masoretic text is probably the youngest of the three, and the *Vorlage* of the Septuagint is closer to the Masoretic text than the Dead Sea Scrolls are, scholars have concluded that the Scrolls represent the oldest form of the text, and are thus the closest we are ever likely to get to the first Hebrew Bible.

Can you tell me a little more about the Masoretic Text?

The name, as I just mentioned, comes from the Masoretes, who were a group of scribes in medieval times. They lived in Egypt late in the first millennium, in the ninth or tenth century A.D. They codified the rules about how to copy a manuscript, adding numerous marginal notes, called *masorah,* to the Hebrew Bible. These *masorah* usually specified the correct spelling and pronunciation of words, explained editorial decisions, and indicated how the text should be preserved without variations. The Masoretic Text became the standard Hebrew-language text of the Bible.

What is the story behind the Septuagint?

Legend has it that the Hebrew Bible was translated into Greek because the large Jewish communities in Alexandria and in other Greek-speaking cities in Egypt demanded a Bible in their own language. So Ptolemy II, ruler of Egypt in the third century B.C., arranged for Jewish scholars from Jerusalem to come to Alexandria.

Originally, the number of scholars was 72, corresponding to the number of members in the Sanhedrin, the Jewish supreme court and legislative body during Roman rule. The tradition is that seventy of them (*septuaginta* is Latin for "seventy") were locked in separate cells, and each wrote a translation. It turned out that each translation was identical to the others!

We do not need to accept this story as literal fact, but the premise is that a substantial group of Jewish scholars undertook this task of translating the Hebrew Bible into Greek sometime in the third century B.C. Their work continued for 100 or maybe 200 years, until all books in the Hebrew Bible were translated into Greek.

Later, the New Testament writings were added to the Bible of Greek-speaking Christians, but the term "Septuagint" applies strictly to the Old Testament portion of that Bible. In fact, the Old Testament that most early Christians knew was the Septuagint, not the Bible in Hebrew.

If you see a quote from the Old Testament in the New — that is, if you look at the original Greek of the New Testament — most often you find that the quote is from the Septuagint. Before the New Testament was written or canonized, the Septuagint simply was "the Bible" to most early Christians.

What do the Dead Sea Scrolls have to do with Islam?

Although the Qur'an doesn't quote from the Hebrew Bible like the Christian New Testament does, the Qur'an does share some of the same history that is recorded in the biblical books found among the Scrolls. The first five books of the Hebrew Bible, called the Torah, tell of Noah, Abraham, Moses, Lot, and other individuals who also appear in the Qur'an. Therefore the Torah not only contains the earliest historic records of Judaism and Christianity, but also of Islam.

The Greatest Archaeological Find of the Twentieth Century: A 2,000-Year-Old Time Capsule

How many Scrolls were there originally, before decay and dispersal set in?

I can't give you an exact number, but there have been estimates that as many as 900 manuscripts were originally in the eleven caves on the northwest shore of the Dead Sea, although only a small fraction has survived. Picture, therefore, a library with 900 volumes. That may not seem like much by modern standards, but recall that each Scroll was immensely valuable, having been copied by hand on costly materials.

What's more, it's possible that a catastrophe overtook the Qumrânites before they were able to conceal their entire library, so they may have had even more volumes that were never found in the caves.

When were the Dead Sea Scrolls discovered?

The first discovery of scrolls in the caves of Qumrân was in 1947. Two young Bedouin discovered them while looking for a lost sheep or goat that strayed into a cave near the northwest-

The Scrolls were discovered by two Taʿmireh Bedouin goatherds, when Muhammed ed-Dhib (right) threw a rock into a cave and heard something shatter. At first frightened away, he returned later and found ten clay jars, one of which contained ancient writings. (John C. Trever)

ern shore of the Dead Sea at Wâdi Qumrân, a gorge cut in the limestone cliffs by winter rains. One of the boys threw a rock into the cave and heard the sound of pottery breaking. The boys ran away, scared of hyenas or *djinni* (magical spirits or "genies"), but one of them, Muhammed ed-Dhib, later returned, lured by thoughts of buried treasure.

He found the first batch of Dead Sea Scrolls. Later this cave became known as Cave 1; it yielded seven Scrolls, which Muhammed ed-Dhib sold to an antiquities dealer in Jerusalem, Khalil Iskander Shahin, whose nickname was Kando.

As word of the initial discovery spread, the wasteland was invaded by other Bedouin, who searched thousands of caves. Some of them found scroll fragments, which they circulated from tent to tent — stored in cigarette, shoe, or film boxes, and sometimes wrapped in wool or tissue paper, with gummed paper to fix major cracks. In addition to the documents found near Qumrân, another batch was found about twelve miles to the southwest in the Wâdi Murabba'ât, and still others emerged from caves known only to Bedouin further south along the Dead Sea. The Bedouin sold the scrolls to antiquities dealers, and the dealers in turn sold them to the archaeologists and scholars.

Because the nation of Jordan controlled the area of the Dead Sea at the time, the agency officially responsible for the Dead Sea Scrolls was the Jordanian Department of Antiquities. However, some of the Scrolls were bought by the Israeli scholar Eleazar L. Sukenik of Hebrew University, who had negotiated directly with the Bedouin. In addition, the Syrian Orthodox Metropolitan of Jerusalem had bought some of the Cave 1 Scrolls from Kando. He allowed John Trever, who was studying at the American School of Oriental Research (ASOR) in Jerusalem, to photograph three of his Scrolls.

At that point, neither ASOR nor the Hebrew University knew that the other institution had seen, let alone purchased or photographed, any of the Scrolls. The first public announcement of the discovery was on April 11, 1948, by Professor Millar Burrows, the director of ASOR. Two weeks later, on April 26, Professor Sukenik revealed the existence of the Hebrew University's collection. Working out how the Scrolls have been circulated and owned has been both a major challenge as well as an achievement.

You've actually worked with a Dead Sea Scroll fragment. How did that happen and what was that like?

Frank Cross and I were students of William Foxwell Albright at The Johns Hopkins University. Sometime in January 1948, Albright summoned us into his office to see photos of ancient biblical texts he had received from John Trever, who was working at the American School of Oriental Research in Jerusalem. Albright was very excited about these photos — primarily the Isaiah Scroll — and said, "This is the real thing!" We immediately went to work authenticating and dating the Scrolls. Albright was primarily interested in the script and spelling, which was unusual in the Scrolls. Almost immediately, he said, "First century B.C.," making it by far the oldest extensive manuscript of the Hebrew Bible we have.

In time, the Dead Sea Scrolls editorial committee, a group of specialists on the Hebrew Bible, divided the Scrolls among themselves, as I mentioned earlier. It was thanks to my former classmate, Frank Cross, that I was included. The committee assigned Leviticus to me, but they told me I could have access to all of the Scrolls. It was a very difficult job reading the pictures and negatives, but it was an incredible experience.

The Leviticus Scroll was several feet long and missing its lower third. But for a manuscript 2,000 years old, it was very well preserved and not difficult to read. The script was unusual, but readable after I got used to it. As I mentioned earlier, it was in paleo-Hebrew, a script that the Essenes held to be sa-

Identifying fragments and piecing them together into a manuscript is the ultimate jigsaw puzzle. Here a member of the Scrolls team sorts some of the 15,000 fragments found in Qumrân Cave 4. (Estate of John Allegro)

cred. The Scroll covers about 12 of the 27 chapters of Leviticus, the latter part of the book, so it's not complete; but about two-fifths of the manuscript is better than nothing.

Where are the Scrolls now?

Eight of the Scrolls are housed in Israel at a museum called the Shrine of the Book. The Shrine is a remarkable building, two-thirds submerged in a pool of water to keep the inside temperature cool, and with a roof shaped like a clay pot from Qumrân. This is the best home for the Scrolls when they're not on exhibition elsewhere. Most of the rest are at the Israel Antiquities Authority (IAA) State Collections. A few Scrolls are in Jordan and Europe.

Since there's no point in storing Scrolls that don't exist,

After sorting, members of the original Scrolls team place fragments between sheets of glass for preservation. (Estate of John Allegro)

funds must always be raised for their conservation. To this end, the IAA allows the Scrolls to tour to various museums around the world, with exhibitions usually lasting from three to six months.

Is it significant that the Dead Sea Scrolls' discovery in 1947 coincided with an apocalyptic date: shortly after the Second World War and a year before the State of Israel was proclaimed in 1948?

Every age is potentially apocalyptic, and people of every generation tend to exaggerate the apocalyptic features of their own era. So no matter when the Scrolls were found, the discovery would have created the same stir. After sixty years of active discussion that still continues unabated, the Scrolls call our attention to the past rather than to the future end of the world.

This is not to say that the Essenes were not concerned with the end of the world. They were. My colleague Frank Cross calls the Essenes "an apocalyptic community" or "a *Heilsgemeinschaft*" (that is, a community seeking salvation), waiting for their version of the final battle between the forces of good and the forces of evil. Their apocalyptic focus emerged from their experience of persecution. It reminded them that they, as the Children of Light, were on God's side and that God ultimately wins. And it helped them visualize their oppressors' doom.

What did archaeologists find when they entered the caves at Qumrân for the first time?

Scrolls from Cave 1 had been in large terracotta jars, and Cave 11 was relatively sheltered, but Cave 4 truly looked like the aftermath of a war. The surprise in Cave 4 was that tens of thousands of fragments (the official report stated 15,000) had all suffered serious damage and were strewn about under three feet of accumulated debris. These Scrolls were clearly moved at the last minute under great threat when the Romans came through on their way to the siege of Jerusalem.

Most likely, the Essenes originally kept all the Scrolls in

In the late 1940s marketplace, dealers sold the first Scroll fragments by centimeters (1 Jordanian pound per centimeter).
(Estate of John Allegro)

their Scriptorium, a large hall that served as their library and on-site copying center. There must have been a librarian to keep track of all the documents. But they moved everything into Cave 4 for preservation because they were under attack and needed to secure their valuables for safekeeping, expecting to return to their hoard when the danger had passed. But it never did.

How has technology improved our ability to study the Scrolls?

For example, infrared photography allows us to read Scrolls that are weathered, soiled, or otherwise unreadable, and multi-spectral imaging enables us to read fragile Scrolls that are still rolled. To sort out 100,000 fragments, DNA analysis

Manuscript Conservation

Every generation uses the best technology available, but subsequent generations not only discover better techniques, but also discover the errors of their predecessors and are forced to reverse the damage.

1950s   Clear tape to cover lettering (ruins the manuscript because it will never come off)

Scrolls displayed behind glass (darkens the papyrus irreversibly).

1990s   Undo the damage caused by the previous work (using Goo-Gone® to remove sticky tape; a Dust Buster® to vacuum dirt; bleach to remove dark stains)

Future   Even more perfected, perhaps high tech, methods reverse damage caused by the "primitive" technologies of the 1950s and 1990s

matches individual pieces of Scrolls, and computer programs match edges of torn Scrolls. Chemical analysis of the Scroll jars determines the source and location of the clay, while carbon-14 dating precisely dates the Scrolls. All of these recent developments allow us to read and preserve the Scrolls to a greater degree.

Of course, it's important to remember that few of these technologies were available when the Scrolls were first discovered. But even with only our eyes and brains as tools, we learned a lot!

Will more Scrolls be discovered?

There are hundreds, even thousands of caves in the area where the Scrolls were found. Most of them have been searched and explored by Bedouin and archaeologists. Still, chances are that more fragments will surface, but it's mostly a matter of luck. Many people suspect that other Scrolls have been found and are in the possession of private individuals. Every so often, rumors crop up that some are for sale for very large amounts and that discreet negotiations are taking place to procure them — but while the rumors surface, I don't think any additional Scrolls have. In fact, no new Scrolls have appeared on the antiquities market since the 1967 Six-Day War, when the Israeli army seized the Temple Scroll from its hiding place in the East Jerusalem home of the dealer Kando. (He was later compensated with $105,000.) The majority of us do believe that sooner or later, new materials will be found, as has happened in the past. But we don't know when. And for now, we have plenty to keep us busy.

The Ancient Book Club

What can you tell us about the books found among the Scrolls?

From the Hebrew Bible, we have fragments of every book except Esther. The most famous discovery is the (nearly) complete text of the book of Isaiah. We also have extensive passages from non-biblical books, too numerous to mention, that contain laws, prayers, blessings, hymns, and wisdom literature. As you may have gathered, the Essenes' reading list was obsessively religious, encompassing biblical, apocryphal (non-canonical), apocalyptic (revealing the end), and liturgical (ritualistic) works. Thinking of themselves as people of a new covenant with God, they were preoccupied with ritual purity that would guarantee their victory over evil forces in the imminent final battle.

As I mentioned earlier, when people refer to the "Dead Sea Scrolls," they often have in mind the sectarian documents that are unique to Qumrân, such as the Manual of Discipline, the Damascus Document, the War Scroll, the Thanksgiving Psalms, the *pesharim,* the Genesis Apocryphon, the Copper Scroll, and the Temple Scroll. I'll tell you about each of these briefly.

The Manual of Discipline explains the community's purpose, initiation rites, theology, and penal codes. It was the guidebook for the *maśkîl,* or master instructor, whose job was "to instruct and teach all the Sons of Light about the generations of all humanity, each according to the kinds of spirits they possess and their deeds in their lifetime."

The Damascus Document is a supplemental rulebook in two parts. Part One exhorts the community to meditate on the lessons of Israel's history to avoid the fate of the wicked apostates, and Part Two is a Constitution that regulates membership.

The War Scroll contains instructions for the final battle of history between the "Sons of Light" (the people of Qumrân) and the "Sons of Darkness" ("profane" Maccabean Jews) at the end of time.

The Thanksgiving Psalms are a prayerbook whose songs and hymns acknowledge human sinfulness and praise the righteous God for delivering the community from tribulation. Many of these hymns begin with "I thank you, O Lord," which gives the Scroll its name.

The *pesharim* or commentaries interpret passages from the Psalms and the Prophets, finding hidden meanings that make the text directly relevant to the historical and social situation of the Qumrân community. The best-known of these is the *pesher* on Habakkuk, one of the seven scrolls discovered in Cave 1 by Muhammed ed-Dhib. The author of this *pesher* found a reference in the book of Habakkuk to a real-life confrontation between the so-called Wicked Priest and the community's Teacher of Righteousness (more on both these characters later), an event that was vividly etched into the community's memory.

The Genesis Apocryphon embellishes the canonical stories of the book of Genesis. In doing so, it resembles somewhat the Jewish *Midrash,* which is literature meant to explain the underlying significance of a Bible text. For example, the Genesis Apocryphon goes into greater detail about Sarah's beauty and Abraham's sojourn in Egypt.

The name of God (YHWH) was so sacred to the Essenes that, in the Scrolls, it was the only word written in a more ancient form of Hebrew script.

𐤉𐤄𐤅𐤄 (A) The Tetragrammaton as it appears in the Dead Sea Scrolls, written in the ancient paleo-Hebrew script.

יהוה (B) The Tetragrammaton in the square letters of the standard "Aramaic" script used in writing Hebrew.

The Copper Scroll is a plaque, made of copper as you might guess, that is rolled to look like two scrolls. It lists 64 locations where treasure is supposedly buried around the Dead Sea region.

The last major sectarian document is the Temple Scroll, which makes the Bible's purity codes and other regulations even more strict.

What does the Essenes' library say about their interests?

We have already noted their religious streak. Since they kept both mainstream Jewish books and sectarian books, we can say that the Essenes were mainstream Jews with particular interests. Their canon of authoritative works was accepted by the rabbis and the high priest in Jerusalem, the final authority. But in addition to these, they kept books of particular interest to them relating to their order of discipline and the climactic battle that they believed would finish off the world.

Frank Cross once said that it was more valuable to have fragments of a cross-section of the whole Hebrew Bible than to have complete manuscripts of only two or three books. Which would you prefer?

I would say we might as well be happy with what we have and not hope for something else.

Besides, we have a substantial representation of both fragments and complete books. We have all kinds of fragments, but we also have complete copies of the books of Samuel and Isaiah. The Samuel Scroll is a very important discovery because it preserves a Hebrew text closer to the Septuagint, the Greek translation of the Hebrew Bible we discussed earlier, than to the Masoretic text. It helps us to see that, in the case of the book of Samuel, the Septuagint almost certainly preserves the better and more original text. With this information, our translations of the Bible can be made more accurate.

Of course, we need to keep in mind that "complete" Scrolls are also fragmentary. Deterioration over the years has left even large, continuous sections full of holes.

Can you tell us more about the books that were found as complete (or nearly complete) manuscripts?

Again, "complete" is a relative term because none of the Scrolls is entirely complete. Of the seven or eight relatively "complete" manuscripts from Cave 1, the best preserved is the great Isaiah Scroll, which contains nearly the entire text of what we know today as the book of Isaiah. In the Isaiah Scroll, some short passages are missing, especially at the beginning and end, where a scroll is most liable to wear and tear.

The Isaiah Scroll testifies that the book was copied faithfully by Jewish scribes throughout the centuries, and proves that the text of Isaiah was stabilized by the second century B.C.. Before this discovery, our oldest copy of Isaiah dated to A.D. 895.

Then there's the Commentary (otherwise known as the *Pesher*) on Habakkuk, which covers the first two chapters of that book. We also have the entire Manual of Discipline, which contains the rules for the Qumrân community. The so-called Genesis Apocryphon, written in Aramaic, is also nearly complete. Other nearly complete scrolls include the War Scroll (whose full name is the Order of the War Between the Children of Light and the Children of Darkness), and a sectarian book of Thanksgiving Psalms. The Leviticus Scroll, which is the one written in paleo-Hebrew script, is not complete, but a large, nearly continuous portion of the book is preserved.

Which books were "best-sellers" at Qumrân?

Three books were the most popular — at least they seem to have been copied the most. Isaiah and Deuteronomy compete for first place, with 12 and 14 surviving manuscripts, respectively. Next comes the book of Psalms, with ten discovered copies. After these, there are also eight copies of the Scroll of the Twelve Prophets (what today we call the "Minor Prophets," the twelve that come after Daniel in Christian Bibles).

The Essenes felt they were living in the age when the end-time prophecies would come true, and the clues could be found in these books. If read with the right eyes, these three books offered the most important predictions of the future — to quote the Commentary on Habakkuk, "all of the secrets of the words of his servants, the prophets."

It's telling that Isaiah, Deuteronomy, and Psalms were also

the favorites of the writers of the New Testament, to judge from the relative number of quotes from these books in the New Testament. Like the Essenes, the early Christians were messianically- and apocalyptically-inclined; but they believed the messiah had come in the person of Jesus.

Why Deuteronomy?

What I just said about predictions doesn't really apply to Deuteronomy, which has very few, although the ones it does have are important. Deuteronomy was important to the Essenes because of its emphasis on the role of Moses. Moses, you may remember, led the new Israelite nation out of slavery in Egypt and through the wilderness for 40 years, and also recorded the Ten Commandments. The Dead Sea community saw itself as a new people called out of the relative "slavery" of mainstream Jewish life, a people who alone kept faith with the Law that Moses handed down.

The predominant expectation among the Essenes was that in the last days three apocalyptic figures would appear: a prophet like Moses, a high priest from the line of Zadok, and the anointed king of the House of David. Therefore, the Essenes were drawn to passages such as Deuteronomy 18:18, wherein God promises Moses that he "will raise up a prophet like you" for the Israelites in latter days.

The Jewish religion saw numerous parallels between Moses and the prophet Elijah. The Essenes were expecting a "third Moses" who would be like Elijah, just as Elijah had resembled Moses. In fact, the Essenes were lucky to have Elijah, since Moses was so sacred to them that they would not have dared to compare anyone with him directly, not even the Great Prophet of the final days.

Why were the Psalms so popular at Qumrân?

The Essenes combed the Hebrew Scriptures to find clues to understanding their community's social and historical situation. Among the different categories of Psalms, the most popular ones in Qumrân were the so-called Royal Psalms. They longed for a king from the line of David to lead them to victory over their Roman occupiers.

Thus they interpreted the Royal Psalms messianically, as prophecies of a figure who would restore the kingly line of David. This figure would be designated by God through a prophet and acknowledged and confirmed as king by the high priest.

Why Isaiah?

Running through the entire book of Isaiah is a messianic theme that captured the Essenes' imagination. Most of the messianic passages are in the first part of Isaiah, especially the familiar chapters 7, 9, and 11. However, the most important is Isaiah 61:1: "The spirit of God is upon me because he has anointed me to preach the gospel to the poor. He has sent me to proclaim release to the captives and recovery of sight to the blind, to set free those who are downtrodden, to proclaim the favorable year of the Lord." Only a king had the authority to proclaim release to captives and relief to the downtrodden. (The Hebrew word for "release," *d'ror*, is also translated "Jubilee," a "sabbatical" period mandated in Israelite law for freeing slaves and canceling debts.) Throughout history, people have been on the lookout for the beginning of a new age, and a messianic figure to bring it. The Essenes were no different.

Why is Esther absent?

It may be purely accidental. Because Queen Esther is mentioned elsewhere in the Dead Sea Scrolls, we know that the Essenes were aware of her. However, even some of the early rabbis doubted whether the book of Esther should be included in the canon, since it is the only book of the Hebrew Bible in which the name of God doesn't appear.

If, in fact, the Essenes rejected the book, however, the absence of God's name was probably not the reason. Rather, the Essenes, with their ascetic lifestyle, probably abhorred the Feast of Purim, which is the holiday for which Esther provides the legendary background. Purim is the one Jewish holiday when drinking wine to excess, while perhaps not encouraged, is not exactly frowned upon, either.

The absence of God's name from the book is really a secondary phenomenon. The primary phenomenon is the nature of the Feast of Purim. The Jews believed that the name of God should only be said while sober. Profanity could be avoided by omitting the name of God so the entire book could be safely read. If Purim were not such a rollicking feast, such precautions would have been unnecessary. And "rollicking" would scarcely have described the atmosphere at Qumrân at any time of the year.

Show Me the Money:
Buried Treasure and Other Mysteries

How much would a Scroll fragment sell for on eBay?

When Bedouin treasure-hunters first started selling Scroll fragments in 1947, the Dominican Fathers of the École Biblique and the Director of the Jordanian Department of Antiquities, G. Lankester Harding, were paying a Jordanian pound for a square centimeter, which wasn't very much — only about $1.75 per square centimeter of inscribed surface. I remember that prices soon rose to $3 or $4 a square centimeter in the 1950s. Today, a complete manuscript would run into the millions. The touring Scrolls, for example, are insured for $5-10 million.

Fortune hunters would want me to ask whether there were treasure maps among the Scrolls. So were there?

The Copper Scroll, which got its name because it really is made of beaten, oxidized copper stamped as though it were papyrus — by a clumsy scribe at that — lists 64 hiding places of treasures made of gold, silver, and other precious metals. But no gold-diggers have gotten rich yet. In fact, not a single item has been found, and not many of the places have been identified.

Because the amount of wealth recorded is incredible — over 200 tons! — the Copper Scroll might just be a piece of folklore. On the other hand, some scholars speculate that the Copper Scroll is a genuine record of treasures that the Essenes took from the Herodian Temple before everything was burned or taken by the Romans in A.D. 70. It's possible that the Essenes escaped Jerusalem carrying these treasures into the desert.

Coins were excavated from the site, but why would they be necessary if Qumrân was a self-sufficient commune?

Total isolation from what they perceived to be the wicked world may have been the Essenes' ideal, but the reality was that, to some extent, the community must have depended on outside sources for certain commodities.

We infer from the Damascus Document that groups of Essenes lived outside of Qumrân in larger, more secular communities while preserving their own community's structure and discipline. Such groups would certainly have had economic dealings with the larger society.

It is worth remembering, too, that the Manual of Discipline, which was the rulebook for the Qumrân community, required that initiates into the community surrender all their possessions. Certainly that entailed quantities of cash, which the community's leaders may have set aside for later use.

Have the Dead Sea Scrolls solved any biblical riddles?

There is a little mystery in Daniel 5, the famous chapter about the handwriting on the wall, that the Dead Sea Scrolls can help us solve. In this story, you might remember, a mysterious hand writes four words on the wall, *mene, mene, tekel, parsin*. Many Bible scholars believe the three words represent three different coins. The first one, mentioned twice, is a *mina*, a very large coin weighing 60 pounds; then *tekel* is a shekel, a much smaller coin; and *parsin* is a half-mina.

The question "What do they symbolize?" has always been ominous, because shortly after the time in which the story is set, the king of Babylon was killed and the Babylonian dynasty came to an end. Prior to the discovery of the Scrolls, scholars had suspected that the three coins, represented by the three words, stand for three successive kings. So the question is, "Who are they?"

Because of its enormous weight, the first coin can only be Nebuchadnezzar, who was truly a giant among kings. He conquered Judah and Jerusalem, and he constructed several monumental buildings in Babylon. The book of Daniel contains numerous stories about the prophet Daniel's interactions with King Nebuchadnezzar. The second coin, the shekel, must stand for the least important ruler of the three, and now, thanks to the Scrolls, we know who he is: the last ruler of the worldwide Babylonian Empire, Nabonidus. His name was totally lost in the Hebrew Bible, but he appears frequently in Babylonian and Persian records.

Nabonidus spent most of his reign in self-imposed exile in Arabia as a devotee of the moon god, Sin, while neglecting the chief god of Babylon, Marduk. As a result, the reputation of Nabonidus was very poor among his own people (hence his being symbolized by such a puny coin). Perhaps rightly, many thought that he was more than just a little crazy.

Daniel 4 presents a story about a crazy Babylonian king, but in that story, the king is Nebuchadnezzar. Scholars long suspected that the story of the crazy king originally featured Nabonidus, but that Nabonidus had eventually been replaced by a far more famous predecessor.

The Dead Sea Scrolls effectively confirm this theory by giving us a fascinating document known as the Prayer of Nabonidus. In this prayer, Nabonidus praises the God of Israel for healing him of an unnamed disease. Just as Nebuchadnezzar is healed by Daniel, the healing of Nabonidus in this Scroll comes at the hands of an anonymous Jewish diviner.

Nabonidus also acknowledges his earlier foolishness in worshiping idols of wood and stone, just as Nebuchadnezzar does in Daniel. The parallels are striking, and they confirm that by the time Daniel was written, Nabonidus had been pushed out of his own story by Nebuchadnezzar.

So *mene, mene, tekel, parsin* represents a sequence that begins with mighty Nebuchadnezzar, continues with wimpy Nabonidus, and ends with Belshazzar, the heir who reigned in Babylon during Nabonidus's self-imposed exile. The *parsin* coin indicates that Belshazzar was a much better ruler than his father, but still only half as good a king as Nebuchadnezzar.

Because of historical circumstances, half as good as Nebuchadnezzar would just not cut it, since a mighty rival to Babylon had arisen to the north and east. In Babylonian tradition, the reason the Persian King Cyrus was able to take Babylon without a fight was that Nabonidus had displeased Marduk by failing to honor him properly. No matter how good a king he might have been, Belshazzar simply could not overcome a handicap of that size.

Perhaps the only bright side of all this for the Babylonians is that Nebuchadnezzar saves face. The Prayer of Nabonidus proves that Nebuchadnezzar may never have been a lunatic after all.

The Dead Sea Is Deathly Hot . . .
Why There?

Why didn't 2,000 years of the extreme heat of the Dead Sea region destroy the Scrolls?

The key fact about the desert is not the temperature, but the lack of humidity. Archaeologists have found that Egypt, with its hot, dry air, is the best place to preserve scrolls, whether leather or papyrus. And the climate of the Judean wilderness is a lot like that of Egypt. It's mostly desert, and this is the only reason we have the Scrolls today. Nothing destroys organic material faster than moisture.

Fortunately for us, the Essenes' method of storing documents also contributed to the Scrolls' extraordinary preservation. Many of the Scrolls were placed in clay jars that weren't sealed, but were loosely covered. As the manuscripts deteriorated, they formed a kind of glue that sealed the jars. No one could have predicted this, and it certainly wasn't intentional.

Overview of the Qumrân settlement and the surrounding area, facing northwest. Across the face of the ravine (lower left), which leads to Wâdi Qumrân, are four of the caves where Scrolls were found. (Werner Braun)

Why did the Essenes leave Jerusalem for the Dead Sea?

In the second century B.C., the Essenes rejected the authority of the high priest of the Temple in Jerusalem and fled the city. This "Wicked Priest" became their chief enemy, opposing and persecuting them and pursuing them to Qumrân.

To quote from one of their own Scrolls, the Essenes sought "to separate from the congregation of the men of iniquity in order to become a community in law and in wealth, responsible

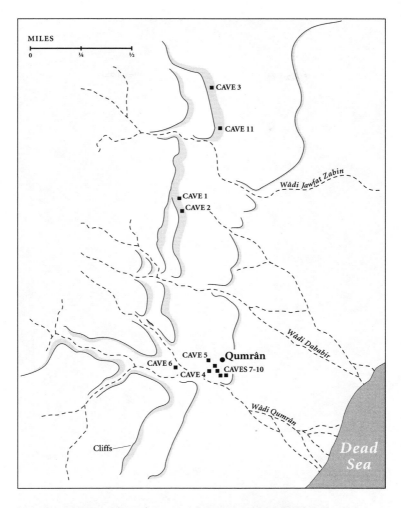

Location of the 11 Qumrân caves. Scholars arbitrarily identify and cata-
logue each Scroll according to Cave number and Scroll number (e.g.,
11Q19 would be Scroll no. 19 from Cave 11) or the name of a book (e.g.,
4QIsaiah would be the Isaiah Scroll from Cave 4).

The first PC. Two thousand years ago the Qumrân Essenes wrapped the Scrolls in linen and stored them in clay jars. (Israel Antiquities Authority)

to the sons of Zadok, the priests who keep the Covenant, and to the majority of the men of the community, who hold fast to the Covenant." They saw themselves as the Children of Light, but the Temple in Jerusalem was in the hands of the Children of Darkness.

Their movement to the Dead Sea had to do with their interpretations of certain prophetic statements from the Hebrew Bible, especially in the major prophets, books like Isaiah, Jeremiah, and Ezekiel. In essence, they believed they were embarking on a Second Exodus to fulfill the New Covenant at the end of the world, withdrawing "from the midst of the habitation of men of iniquity to go into the desert to prepare there the way for [God]."

Why Qumrân?

The site of Qumrân had been settled before. Some evidence suggests that originally it had been Gomorrah, one of the "Cities of the Plain" that God destroyed by fire (Genesis 13:10). A later settlement on the same site, known as the "City of Salt" (Joshua 15:62), was one of the fortress towns of the Judean kings. It's in this same region that David hid out from Saul (1 Samuel 23). But no matter what was there before, when the Essenes arrived the site had lain deserted since the sixth century B.C.

We don't know whether the Essenes knew the history of the site, but their likely reason for settling there is a prophecy in the book of Ezekiel. In Ezekiel 47, the prophet foresees a time when a freshwater river will flow out from the Temple in Jerusalem and down to the Dead Sea. There is a wâdi (a gorge cut in limestone cliffs) that runs down from Jerusalem to the Dead Sea. If you follow it, guess where you come out? Lo and behold, at Qumrân! So despite their self-imposed exile from the Holy City, in a certain sense the Essenes maintained a connection to

Jerusalem, one that they expected would become even more important in the end time.

The Essenes were not deterred by the harshness of the climate or the isolation because they expected their home to be transformed into a paradise, a heaven on earth, in the foreseeable future. Imagine buying real estate in Arizona with the firm expectation that California would sink into the sea in the next big earthquake. Your desert would suddenly turn into highly valuable oceanfront property. This is something like what the Essenes must have imagined.

And the Essenes liked being off the beaten track because it meant their group could expect to be left alone. As far as we can tell, the Essenes were not aggressive. They didn't plan to capture new territories or expand their base. They simply intended to wait for the final act of world history — their ultimate victory over the Children of Darkness.

Did the Essenes foresee the destruction of Jerusalem?

Unlike the gospels, in which Jesus explicitly predicts the destruction of the city and the Temple, the Scrolls of Qumrân are vague about what they expect to happen to Jerusalem. However, the Essenes certainly would not have minded if the Temple were to be destroyed, since they had their own ideas about how it should look, and those ideas did not correspond to what was actually there.

When the Essenes left Jerusalem in the second century B.C., the Temple was a very modest building that the Jews had constructed in the sixth century B.C. upon returning from exile in Babylon. In 20-19 B.C., after the Essenes had been at Qumrân for at least a century, Herod the Great rebuilt the Temple. Needless to say, he did not employ the Essenes as his architects.

However, the Essenes recognized that they lacked temporal power. All they could do was wait for the climactic battle between good and evil, after which they would take possession of Jerusalem and either cleanse or rebuild the Temple according to the specifications in their Temple Scroll.

The Essenes' communal way of life reflected their zealous preoccupation with the dawning new age when they would inherit the New Jerusalem. Though they referred to themselves as the "Congregation of the Poor," they did not expect to be poor forever.

What was their settlement like?

The famous first-century historian Philo of Alexandria remarked that the Essenes lived in an "indescribable community," sharing clothes, rooms, money, and meals. The floor plan of the settlement at Qumrân bears this out.

A large square building, 124 feet on each side, lay at the center of the settlement. Inside this building was a central hall with plaster pillars and a thatched palm roof. Archaeologists have found tableware in this central hall, which indicates that the Essenes probably held their sacred common meals there. To the south and west, more buildings can be found, and on the eastern side of the settlement a long defensive wall emerges from the central building and continues into the wâdi (the gorge) sealing the community off from the east.

Because of the long dry season in Palestine, the ability to move and store water was extremely important. The Essenes built a large maze of water channels in addition to seven cisterns, six small pools, and numerous basins and baths. An aqueduct — which is still intact — carried water from a dam at the foot of a waterfall further up the wâdi.

Some scholars think all the basins were used for baptism, but the basins are very much like water reservoirs, and the Essenes wouldn't bathe or practice baptism in drinking water.

Scribes copied biblical and sectarian scrolls in a room called the Scriptorium ("writing room"). Archaeologists have found benches, tables, and ceramic and bronze inkwells such as this containing the remains of dried ink. (Photo by David Harris, courtesy The Shrine of the Book, Israel Museum)

Most likely, when they needed to perform ritual baptisms, they used water from the Jordan River, which was "living water" in the ritual sense — that is, water that flowed freely in nature and that had not been stored for a prolonged period.

We have also found basalt millstones, silos for grain storage, a bakery, and a pottery studio, all necessary in any relatively self-sufficient community. Most interesting is the Scriptorium, where the excavators found a plaster table and a low bench, even three inkpots with some dried ink. This is where scrolls were copied, and it was probably where the Cave 4 Scrolls originated.

When was the community's last day?

We can't really be sure, since no written records document its demise. All we know is that at some point in the late first century A.D., probably in connection with the First Jewish Revolt against the Romans (A.D. 66-70), the Essenes at Qumrân just vanished.

Most likely they made the mistake of fighting the Romans instead of surrendering. The ruins of their community are encased in layers of ash from a great fire, and in the debris, iron arrowheads have been found, which are a sure sign of Roman legionaries.

Once the community center was destroyed, the Essene movement as a whole went into rapid decline and vanished by the end of the century. After their defeat at Qumrân, they certainly dispersed into Jewish society, but apparently they blended too well and lost their identity. Very few Essenes are mentioned in the records of the First Jewish War, and by the time of the Second War under Bar Kokhba (A.D. 132-135), they had disappeared from history.

Did anyone from their time period record the history of the Essenes?

Not really. The rabbinical literature of the third and fourth centuries A.D. tells us a bit about them. And we glean bits and pieces from other works: the books of the Maccabees; histories by Flavius Josephus such as *The Jewish War;* the *Refutatio omnium haeresium* of Hippolytus; a short notice by Pliny the Elder; and some of the works of Philo of Alexandria. Philo observed: "They not only practice contemplation, but also compose songs and hymns to God in all sorts of meters and melodies." The Dead Sea Scrolls are a credit to Josephus, Pliny, and Philo. The Essenes' records confirm that these major historians were excellent observers, reporting accurately.

Reconstructing the Essenes' history and life is a slow process, but in doing so, we fill in a lost chapter in the development of Jewish and Christian culture.

The End of the World and the Battle Between Good and Evil

When did the Essenes think the world would end? Did they have a specific date in mind?

The end of the world was always *about* to come. The Essenes thought they were living in the last days, and anticipated a final battle between the forces of good (the Children of Light) and those of evil (the Children of Darkness). I mentioned earlier how they used their *Pesharim,* or commentaries, to interpret Scripture in terms of current events, just as many apocalyptic groups have done through the years. (Students of American religious history might remember the Millerites, who expected the world to end in 1844 and, after nothing happened, in 1845.)

The Essenes also gleaned ideas from the book of Daniel, which was a product of the same period. The writer of Daniel had no faith in the Maccabees, the priestly family that was at that time leading a Jewish revolt against foreign rule. He thought that Antiochus, the Syrian emperor who controlled Israel, was the last evil ruler of history, and that God, not the Maccabees, would defeat him and usher in the new age. As it turned out, the Maccabees won a military victory and established a relatively stable, decidedly this-world dynasty. The victory probably disappointed the Essenes, as well as the author of Daniel, but it would not have dissuaded them.

Speaking of specific dates, one book the Essenes used in their calculations was the book of Ezekiel. Ezekiel 4:5 makes reference to a span of 390 years, and when you add 390 to 586 B.C. (the year in which the first Temple of Jerusalem was destroyed), you arrive at 196 B.C. To this the Essenes added a 20-year period mentioned in another one of the Scrolls, called the Damascus Document. These numbers left the end of the world squarely within the Essenes' time. And when it didn't come? They would simply tweak their numbers to come up with another date.

Do the Essenes' prophecies have any relevance for us today, or is it all passé since what they predicted didn't occur?

The people of Qumrân were no more wrong than the New Testament writers, and we give considerable slack to the latter. Paul and the writers of the gospels all expected Jesus' second coming to take place during their lifetimes, and when it didn't, it fell to succeeding generations of Christians to reinterpret certain things that Jesus did and said. The real value of apocalyptic writings such as we find in the Dead Sea Scrolls lies in their applicability to every generation. Human beings always face this crisis, this ominous judgment at the end. The challenge is to respond to it.

By now, most of us do not expect the end of the world immediately because it just hasn't happened all these centuries. But you never know: an errant asteroid might just hit us, as one did 160 million years ago when it wiped out the dinosaurs! So while we shouldn't live in fear, neither is it a good idea to presume we're immortal.

It's clear that the ancient Hebrew prophets as well as the

early Christians expected some dramatic changes, and we would have to say that nothing that corresponded exactly to their expectations happened. Yet both Christianity and Judaism have made similar accommodations and adjustments to the fact that the end did not come.

Who were the Children of Light, and who were the Children of Darkness?

According to the Scroll known as the Manual of Discipline, every person falls into one of these two categories. Clearly, in their own minds, the Essenes were the Children of Light, a class that excluded most of their fellow Jews.

The Manual of Discipline reads, "For God has set these two spirits with equal influence until the end time and has put eternal hatred between their divisions. The deeds of iniquity are an abomination to truth, and an abomination to iniquity are all the paths of truth." It goes on to say that God chose the Children of Light for an eternal covenant, promising them a heavenly realm of glory, health, peace, and light.

The rest of humanity are Sons of Darkness, and they are doomed, as the Scroll attests: "Accursed be you without mercy according to the darkness of your deeds, and may you be damned in the deep darkness of everlasting fire! May God not be gracious to you when you call upon him and not pardon you by wiping away your iniquities! . . . May all the curses of this covenant cling to [the Son of Darkness], and may God set him apart for evil. May he be cut off from the midst of the sons of light in his turning back from God because of his idols and the stumbling-block of his iniquity." And the curse would end in a resounding "Amen, amen!"

The Manual of Discipline paints the righteous as God-fearing, humble, merciful, good, intelligent, wise, zealous, holy, affectionate, pure, and modest. They are promised a long, healthy, and happy life: "As for the visitation of all who walk by it, it will be healing, abundant peace, length of days, fruitfulness of seed [i.e., abundant progeny], together with everlasting blessing and eternal joy in life without end, a crown of glory, and a garment of honor in everlasting light."

The wicked are portrayed as covetous, slack, deceitful, proud, false, cunning, cruel, hypocritical, impatient, frivolous, envious, lustful, blasphemous, blind, deaf, stiff-necked, and heavy-hearted.

Basically, anyone who was not an Essene — a Child or Son of Light — would be purged from existence, destroyed forever by God. And the Essenes — as "merciful" Children of Light — appeared to relish this thought.

Could the Essenes have been wrong about themselves? Doesn't their defeat prove that they were actually Children of Darkness?

Just because the movement faded away does not mean that all of its adherents perished. Unlike the Samaritans, another Jewish sect, the Essenes failed to preserve their communal identity, but many probably moved on to other affiliations. Some might have become Christians; some no doubt blended in with the larger Jewish community.

They were defeated and their movement faded away, to be sure. But to call the Essenes Children of Darkness would be going too far. For one thing, they were clearly observant Jews who lived by the Torah. And for another, "Children of Darkness" is their own term, with its own particular place in their view of the world. If we could speak to them today, no doubt they would still point out that they stood in the legitimate line of Zadok, unlike the illegitimate Maccabees whom they considered to be the Children of Darkness. And the Maccabean line also died out. "Darkness" is always in the eye of the beholder.

How was the settlement at Qumrân destroyed?

Coins recovered at the site give us a timeline for the Essenes' settlement at Qumrân, which can be summarized as follows: it was begun around 125 B.C., destroyed by an earthquake in 31 B.C., rebuilt in 5 B.C., and destroyed by the Tenth Roman Legion in A.D. 68.

The community thrived without interruption during Roman rule, until the first Jewish revolt against Rome, which began in the year A.D. 66. We can reconstruct the final days when Vespasian marched east from Caesarea on the coast, attacking in the south and then in the north before occupying Jericho, from whence he moved on to the Dead Sea. (Josephus tells us that Vespasian tested the water's unusual density by throwing in bound prisoners to see if they would float.) Vespasian's troops destroyed Qumrân in the early summer of A.D. 68.

Apart from squatters during the second Jewish revolt in A.D. 132-135, Qumrân wasn't occupied again until archaeologists camped there in 1951. We don't know whether the Essenes fled the Romans or were slaughtered by them, but we know they didn't have time to evacuate the manuscripts from their hiding place in Cave 4. Ironically, if the Essenes had survived, the manuscripts might not have.

Do we know the identity of the Wicked High Priest?

The identity of the Wicked High Priest has been the subject of a huge debate. The information in the Scrolls is insufficient to identify him. A crucial point about the Wicked Priest is that originally he was a legitimate High Priest. There's a passage in the Commentary on Habakkuk that says he "was called in the name of truth at the beginning of his rise, but when he came to rule over Israel, his heart became haughty." Personally, I take the first part of that quote to mean that in the eyes of the

Essenes, the Wicked Priest, before he was corrupted, was qualified for the job of high priest.

And at the very least that means he was a descendant of Zadok, who was high priest during the reign of King David. That narrows the field, because the last truly Zadokite high priest was Hananiah III (most people use the Greek form of his name, Onias). Hananiah reigned from 196-175 B.C., but he was deposed as the result of political intrigue, and all the high priests after him, although they were in the priestly group as descendants of Moses' brother Aaron, lacked the Zadokite descent. In the eyes of the Essenes, this made them illegitimate.

Most scholars think that the Wicked Priest was one of the Maccabees, the family that liberated Israel from Syrian oppression in the 160s B.C. After their victory against Syria, the sons of this family reigned first as king and then as both king and high priest. The problem with this theory is that the Essenes would not have been able to say about a Maccabee ruler that he was "called according to the name of truth," at least not called *as a priest*, because the Essenes were so very particular about priestly qualifications. A non-Zadokite was a nonstarter as far as they were concerned.

A scenario in which Hananiah is cast as the Wicked Priest fits with what we know about the Essenes and the history of the period. The decades leading up to the Maccabees' war against Antiochus IV, which is narrated in the apocryphal book of 1 Maccabees, were defined by a struggle between religious Jews and those who wanted to take on the trappings of Hellenistic (that is, Greek) culture, known as Hellenizers.

Knowing as we do what purists the Qumrânites were, I consider it likely that they left Jerusalem sooner rather than later, as they saw corruption (i.e., Hellenistic influence) growing in their society and in the politics of the religious establishment. They had a lower tolerance than most people, and like canaries in the coal mine, they croaked first.

Except that they didn't just fall over and die. They took their manuscripts with them (many of the Dead Sea Scrolls represent works that predate the community) into the wilderness and, fortunately for us, began documenting the story of their alienation and the ideas and feelings that blossomed into a distinctively rich spiritual and religious life of their own.

A few decades later, most of the population of Judah reached the same conclusion as the Essenes — namely that Hellenization, the surrender of Jewish identity for the Greek, had gone too far — and they supported the Maccabees in their uprising.

What made the Wicked Priest "wicked" in the Essenes' eyes?

Well, it was bad enough that he persecuted them, but the Essenes may overstate that. If the Wicked Priest really was Hananiah III, his famous visit to Qumrân may have been an attempt to create a more unified front against foreign domination. The problem for rulers with real responsibility is that they must compromise. They can't afford to be purists.

The passage that I referred to in the Commentary on Habakkuk reveals a lot about what the Qumrânites thought about the Wicked Priest. It says that when the Wicked Priest's "heart became haughty . . . he abandoned God and betrayed the precepts because of riches. He stole and heaped up the riches of violent men who had rebelled against God" (1QpHab 8:8-11).

Here you see two principles that are often tangled up in religious institutions: doctrine and money. The Essenes clearly saw the High Priest's wealth as a sign of corruption, of laxity regarding the requirements of Scripture.

Although the Essenes were no doubt sincere in their doctrinal beliefs, one can't help but detect a note of sour grapes in their comment about the Wicked Priest's wealth. The Essenes made a virtue out of necessity by adopting an austere lifestyle in the wilderness, but when they were vindicated in the final battle, they expected to be restored to power, which of course would mean that they would then control the wealth.

Translating Translations
and Copying Copies

When was the Hebrew Bible finished?

Scholars have varying opinions about this; personally, I take a very simple approach. I believe the books of the Hebrew Bible (with one exception) were finished during the Exile, within 20 years of the last date alluded to in the last book. A text draws its life from the writer's experience, and the narrative stops when the experience stops, that is, in the writer's present. Think of a history book written in 1930: you would expect it to cover the events of World War I, but not those of World War II.

The last event described in what I call the Primary History — that is, the books of Genesis through Kings — took place in 560 B.C., namely, the release of the Judahite King Jehoiachin from prison into mere house arrest (2 Kings 25:27-30). Twenty years later, Cyrus issued an edict allowing Judean exiles to return to Jerusalem, but there is not a single word of this in the entire Primary History. Why not? It's a no-brainer: the Primary History had long since been finished.

The second half of the Hebrew Bible was then finished around 400 B.C. The exception that I alluded to earlier is Daniel, which was written about 165 B.C. Notice, however, that in order to be included, Daniel had to present itself as having been written much earlier, in the sixth century B.C., which was well before 400 B.C. and therefore acceptable.

Of course, the Essenes would not have known, or even wondered about, any of this. Like some fundamentalist Jews and Christians today, they would have considered Moses to be the author of the Torah, and all the other books to have come down to them in their original, unaltered form.

How old were the oldest manuscripts of the Hebrew Bible before the Dead Sea Scrolls were discovered?

The oldest complete Hebrew manuscript, the Leningrad Codex in St. Petersburg, goes back to almost A.D. 1008, and some smaller fragments exist going as far back as the first or second century B.C., but we had nothing like this hoard. The Leningrad Codex is certainly old, but it is still 1,000 years younger than the Dead Sea Scrolls.

The Dead Sea Scrolls preserve a much smaller portion of the Hebrew Bible than does the Leningrad Codex, so the latter remains our primary source for the text of the Bible that we read today. But if you have an annotated Bible, you may notice that variant readings from the Dead Sea Scrolls are mentioned in the notes, which improves our reading of the Hebrew Bible.

Can scholars translate every word of the Dead Sea Scrolls, or are there mysterious passages?

Hebrew is a known language, so the words themselves aren't a mystery. However, there are some enigmatic manuscript fragments that are written in a code that appears to be a combination of paleo-Hebrew, Greek, and other scripts. Nothing can help us with the solution; at least nothing has so far. It's possible that someday someone will discover a Rosetta Stone — something that will help us decode the fragments — but until then the codes remain a mystery.

Two documents written in a different cryptic script were thought to contain the Essenes' guarded secrets. But scholars competed to crack the code, and finally, Abbé Józef Milik, a Catholic priest and one of the original Scrolls scholars, deciphered these two documents. The result was not earth-shattering. One manuscript contained astronomical observations from the apocryphal book of 1 Enoch, and the other was an extracanonical "Exposition (or Midrash) of the Book of Moses."

Why are some biblical books divided into two parts?

The three longest books in the Hebrew Bible — Samuel, Kings, and Chronicles — were divided chiefly because their Greek translations were too long to fit onto a reasonably-sized scroll. At the time the Septuagint was written, the codex, or bound book, as we know it had not yet been invented, so scribes had to make do with scrolls. At a very practical level, the maximum length of a scroll is about 36 feet, and even that is too long, especially when you're looking for a reference.

The Greek translations stretched the boundaries because Greek uses more letters than Hebrew. Whereas Hebrew has letters only for long vowels, Greek represents all the vowels, both short and long. I calculated the ratio once: a Greek translation is about 50% longer than its Hebrew original. This explains why the longest books are split.

Jeremiah represents the upper limit of a book that would fit onto a single scroll when translated: 23,000 words in Hebrew. Kings, Samuel, and Chronicles in that order are between 24,000 and 26,000 words. So they each get two scrolls in the Greek. When the switch was made to the codex, or bound book format, the divisions were preserved, even though technically they were no longer necessary. And so we got 1 and 2 Samuel, 1 and 2 Kings, and 1 and 2 Chronicles.

Are there any other ancient copies of the Hebrew Bible that we can compare to the Dead Sea Scrolls?

Well, there's the Samaritan Pentateuch. As I mentioned before, the Samaritans were a religious group who, in the eyes of the Jews, didn't measure up to the standards of Judaism. You probably remember them from Jesus' parable about the Good Samaritan — a story that would have shocked his Jewish listeners because they wouldn't have thought of a Samaritan as "good" in any sense of the word. But the Samaritans had their own Torah, or Pentateuch, and these scrolls are valuable documents because they reflect a separate scribal history.

In a curious way, the Dead Sea Scrolls confirm that the Samaritan Pentateuch is a very reliable, useful text. It has often been criticized for being longer than the standard text of the Torah, but one can argue that longer is better, in the sense of being closer to the original.

The popular view among scholars is that longer manuscripts aren't as good as shorter ones, that scribes introduce errors by adding to texts and expanding on them. But in my judgment, scribes don't add. I think the chief scribal error in transmission is *omission.* There is so much repetition in the Bible that the eye inadvertently skips, which results in a phenomenon called haplography, or the loss of words.

You've been an editor-in-chief for over 50 years, so fill us in. What exactly is haplography?

The word itself comes from the Greek, meaning "writing once." The implication is that one *ought* to be writing twice! The way it happens is that the scribe's eye skips to the same letter or combination of letters further along in the text, with the result that all the words or letters in between do not get copied and, unless another copy of the same passage survives that was transmitted by a more reliable or luckier scribe (or made its way into a translation), the dropped words are lost forever. Thousands of words have been lost from the original text of the Bible this way.

The Samaritan Pentateuch has fewer occurrences of this loss, or haplography, than the standard Masoretic Text does. To me, this suggests that in many places the Samaritan text may offer us a better and more original reading than the Masoretic Text. Of course, each instance of addition or omission must be examined in its own right.

Which of the two texts — the Septuagint (the "Old Testament" in Greek) or the Masoretic Text (the "Old Testament" in Hebrew) — represents a more accurate tradition?

This is a serious issue. On the one hand, the Septuagint reflects an earlier version than the Masoretic Text. The Masoretic Text can't be traced back as far as the Septuagint, and it seems to reflect a number of instances when rabbis had to make hard choices about which particular texts were original and what particular words meant. It also reflects a great deal of haplography — that scribal omission we just talked about.

On the other hand, scholarly attitudes toward the Septuagint have gone through a lot of stages over the years. It has been considered a very accurate, literal rendering of an underlying Hebrew text — and it has been considered a paraphrase of something that doesn't conform to any Hebrew text.

But the more information that comes in, especially from the Dead Sea Scrolls, the more the Septuagint appears to be a literal translation of an original Hebrew text. In fact, it appears

The Septuagint (the Hebrew Bible translated into Greek) in many cases is closer to the original Hebrew than the Hebrew texts that survived. This fragment of a document called Rylands Greek Papyrus 458, showing Deuteronomy 25:1-3, is one of the earliest surviving texts of the Greek Bible (second century **B.C.**). (John Rylands University Library, Manchester)

to be a *very* literal translation, so much so that in many ways it differs from classical Greek. The translators made deliberate efforts to preserve the original syntax, word order, and so forth of the original Hebrew rather than attempt to achieve an attractive style in Greek. Imagine if a book were translated from German or French into English, but without rearranging the sentences to conform to typical English usage. That is somewhat similar to what we encounter in the Septuagint.

But isn't the Bible supposed to be the Word of God? What are these variations you are talking about?

We have categories of errors, but they're all basically the fault of the human eye, which is a very fallible piece of equipment. When scribes are tired, they make mistakes. Haplography, or omissions, and metathesis, or reversing letters, are very common errors. So is dittography, which is simply the repetition of letters, words, or phrases. I think we can explain more textual differences in terms of these kinds of errors rather than by imagining that scribes deliberately altered texts for theological reasons. I'm not a believer in those theories. Scribes were paid to copy. They made more money if they copied faster, or for longer stretches of time without a rest, which led to errors. I doubt the ancient scribes had the potent stimulants we use today to stay awake!

As for deliberate changes in the biblical text? I think those happened much earlier, when the books were being written (as opposed to merely copied) and going through stages of redaction, or editing. This process ended in A.D. 92, when a group of rabbis met in the town of Jamnia to settle once and for all the canon of the Hebrew Bible. After this so-called "Council of Jamnia," the text was fixed. "This is it," they said. "This is the Word of God. No more changes."

In the Scrolls most of the variations from the Bible occur in the commentaries, where the biblical text is repeated, verse by verse, with each verse followed by comments explaining its hidden meaning. In expounding on the passage, the Qumrân commentator often requoted the text with slight variations. So the Commentary on Habakkuk gives us one and sometimes two additional versions of Habakkuk as we have it in the Hebrew Bible. Some of these variants offer intriguing — but ultimately speculative — interpretive possibilities.

The omissions in the Masoretic Text have nothing to do with content. The scribes weren't making conscious changes.

Types of scribal errors

Haplography   Omissions occuring when the scribe skips from one letter or word to the next identical letter or word, skipping the letter or word in between.

"*The* scribe wrote *the* book" becomes "*The* book."

Metathesis   Reversing letters or words.

Dittography   Repetition of letters, words, or phrases.

It's simply that the repetition in the Bible makes opportunities for eye-skips and hence for omission great. Probably 99% of the errors were innocent mistakes of tired scribes.

These errors give scholars in the field of textual studies a lot to talk about. We are always considering every little difference, and this leads to interesting conclusions about what the original reading of a given passage might have been. We have one debate after another, and nothing is really ever settled. But ordinary readers wouldn't notice these small differences that are so exaggerated by scholars. Innocent grammatical errors make relatively little difference for the interpretation and theology of the Bible.

Has the meaning of any passage in the Bible been distorted because of haplography?

The most notorious misprint ever produced was in the so-called "Wicked Bible." The Wicked Bible was an English translation printed in 1631 by the official printer of King Charles I of England, and its notorious misprint is a case of haplography. The seventh commandment appeared without the word "not," so that it read, "Thou shalt commit adultery." The typesetter's eye probably skipped from the "t" at the end of "shalt" to the "t" at the end of "not," with the result that "not" simply dropped out. King Charles fined the printer £300, a lifetime's wages by seventeenth-century standards. And he ordered all 1,000 copies destroyed, although eleven are known to have survived.

But this is an extreme case. Most instances of haplography occur at places in the text where you would expect the human eye to make errors, such as in lists of names and places. In Deuteronomy 7, for example, we are given a list of seven peoples conquered or suppressed by the Israelites: the Hittites, Girgashites, Amorites, Canaanites, Perizzites, Hivites, and Jebusites. Well, variations of that list occur about 30 times throughout the Hebrew Bible, but maybe only once or twice do the scribes manage to copy all seven names. Most often we get six or five or even four.

Why? Every single name in the list begins with the same definite article, and ends with the same letters. The potential for eye-skipping is tremendous. But the omission of one or two of these names from a list isn't cause for theological concern.

Can any translation of the Hebrew Bible ever succeed in conveying the original message?

The many Bible versions available run the entire spectrum in terms of theory and practice in translation. Some translators prefer a very smooth, attractive English rendering of the Hebrew — almost more of a paraphrase than a literal translation. These translators believe that if the original message was elegant and attractive in its source language, it should be that way as well in the language into which it is translated.

Other translators take the opposite approach. Their English is more Hebrew than English because they feel it is important to represent the word order and special features of biblical Hebrew. This "Hebrew English" is a strain on English in a deliberate attempt to make a non-Hebrew reader get some of the flavor of the original language, to help them think the way the original readers of the book might have thought.

These approaches, and all approaches in between, are worthy experiments, none of which succeeds completely. For personal reading, it's probably best to choose the Bible translation that you're most comfortable with. But there is a message here: if you really want to get the feel of an original text, learn the language! If a university seems daunting, why not find a Hebrew class in your local synagogue?

What If the Bible
Is Just Another Fragment?
A Primer on Textual Criticism

In the light of the discovery of so many non-biblical and yet decidedly religious works at Qumrân, how can we be sure we have the complete Hebrew Bible?

The people who put together the Bible as we know it were very concerned with completeness. Their decisions were not random or haphazard. I believe that the Bible was put together around 400 B.C., well before the time of the Essenes at Qumrân, and that we can glimpse the compilers' intentions by examining the Bible's structure.

If we do that, and we find meaningful patterns that are simply too intricate to be coincidental, then we can say that "the Bible" already existed as a concept by the time of Qumrân, and that the non-biblical works found at Qumrân never had a serious chance of becoming Scripture.

The first part of the Bible's two halves is what I named the Primary History: the five books of the Torah (Genesis, Exodus, Leviticus, Numbers, Deuteronomy) plus the four books of the Former Prophets (Joshua, Judges, Samuel, and Kings). Samuel and Kings each count as one book; their division into two books each was due merely to the physical limitations on the length of a scroll.

We often think of the five books of the Torah as a unit, distinct from Joshua through Kings. But the stories of Genesis point at least as far forward as Joshua, and, in my opinion, they even foreshadow the narration of Kings. Cutting the narrative off sooner, even though it has been done for thousands of years, violates an artistic and philosophical unity. This is the first half of the Hebrew Bible, the Primary History.

What about the second half?

You read my mind. To match and supplement the Primary History, we have the second half of the Hebrew Bible, which consists of the Latter Prophets (Isaiah, Jeremiah, Ezekiel, and the Scroll of the Twelve or "Minor" Prophets) and the Writings (everything that's left). The single most important numerical fact about the Hebrew Bible is that *these two halves match in terms of the number of words* (in Hebrew, of course, not necessarily in translation)! They're within 1/10 of 1% of each other, and that tells you something. It shows that somebody planned it and that it didn't just happen.

But in order to get these two equal halves you have to exclude the book of Daniel from the Writings. Rather than a drawback, this is a plus for my theory of the Bible's original structure. Why exclude Daniel? Because, as 98% of scholars agree, Daniel is uniquely a product of the late Hellenistic period (the second century B.C.). Everything else in the Bible is from the Persian period (539-325 B.C.) or earlier.

If we remove Daniel, here is the Bible at 400 B.C.: first half, 150,000 words; second half, 150,000 words. Those are round figures, and I don't recall the exact ones right now, but the difference between the two totals is less than 300 words. That's 300 words out of 300,000. Is a 99.9% match close enough?

If this doesn't show "intelligent design," then I don't know what does! Somebody with a brain arranged the Bible symmetrically to show something. What were they trying to show? The definitive Word. Totality and perfection.

Then someone stuffed Daniel into the canon and distorted this perfection, adding 5,000 words. Daniel is a bump, an addition, an aberration in the perfect order. A lot of people would say it shouldn't be in there, but that's a different story.

Are there additional clues that reveal how the Hebrew Bible was structured?

Yes. Some of this may get a little confusing, but try to follow along. Each of the Bible's two halves is also internally divided: five books plus four; then four books plus five. The first half (the Primary History) has the Torah (five books) and the Former Prophets (four); the second half has the Latter Prophets (four books — remember that the Minor Prophets, since they all fit onto one scroll, count as only one "book") and the Writings (whose five major books are Chronicles, Psalms, Job, Proverbs, and Ezra/Nehemiah, which again count as one "book"). That gives us 18 books.

All that's left in the Writings is the Five *Megillot,* or "little scrolls": Ruth, Song of Songs, Ecclesiastes, Lamentations, and Esther. That brings us to 23.

The whole structure is full of mirroring patterns; for example, the three major prophets relate to the Book of the Twelve (the Minor Prophets) in the same way that the three patriarchs (Abraham, Isaac, Jacob) relate to the Twelve Tribes of Israel.

The total number of books, 23 (remember, this is all without Daniel), is also significant. One of the acrostic Psalms begins each line with the next letter of the Hebrew alphabet, which has 22 letters. But then it throws in an extra line beginning with "P." Why is this? Well, with an odd number of letters, you can have not only a first and a last letter, you can also have a middle one. The first letter is Aleph (א), the last is that extra "P" (Peh, פ), and the middle letter is the twelfth from the regular order, Lamed (ל). The letters Aleph, Lamed, and Peh (א, ל, פ) spell the name of the first letter, Aleph.

In the Hebrew mindset, the letter Aleph stands for perfection. The first letter of the alphabet contains the idea of all the letters, and the letters themselves stand for all of reality that can be represented in thought or language. After the exile of the Jews, when they no longer had a homeland or a Temple around which to orient their identity, the 23 letters of David's acrostic psalm, like the 23 books of the Hebrew Bible, became the symbolic substitute for the land, the nation, for everything that had been lost. For this book, they could live.

In Ezra/Nehemiah, the book that tells the end of the biblical story (and the last in the Hebrew order of the books), Ezra reads the Torah aloud to the assembled people at the Water Gate in Jerusalem, starting at the beginning. At the very end of the same book, Nehemiah's last words are "Remember me, O my God, for good" *(zokra li elohai l'tovah)*. That brings us around full circle to the first chapter of Genesis, which is dominated by the words "God" *(elohim)* and "good" *(tov)*.

However, the words are slightly changed in Nehemiah's prayer: instead of *elohim* (God) it's *elohai* (my God), which in Hebrew is one letter shorter. And instead of *tov*, Nehemiah uses *tovah*, which in Hebrew is one letter longer and is also feminine rather than masculine. The *elohim* and *tov* of Genesis 1 and the *elohai* and *tovah* of Nehemiah 12 form complementary wholes that signify totality and perfection: "male and female," "east to west," "A to Z."

This locks the beginning and the end together in a perfect circle: in the beginning you have "God" and "good," and in the end you have "God" and "good." This is what the whole Bible is about.

Why the fascination with numbers?

A fascination with numbers is not unique to the ancient Israelites. It's characteristic of humans in general. The pattern begins with the human body, which is bilaterally symmetrical. For another example, consider the Egyptian pyramids, with their amazing symmetry. Just like the architects of the pyramids wanted to make sure that what they built was ordained by God and reflected perfection, so the makers of the Hebrew Bible wanted their sacred writings to do the same.

Of course, there are different ways to arrive at numerical perfection. The ancient Jewish historian, Josephus, had the perfection of the Hebrew alphabet in mind when he reduced the 24 books of the Hebrew Bible (that total of 24 *includes* Daniel, which Josephus did not know was a later insertion) down to 22, the number of letters in the Hebrew alphabet. He did this by claiming that Ruth was really just a part of Judges and that Lamentations was part of Jeremiah.

By now you're probably gathering that letters can be just as important as numbers. Alphabets symbolize totality, infinity, unity — because everything in the universe can be represented by words, which are specific combinations of letters. In the New Testament, when the author of Revelation has Jesus say, "I am the Alpha and the Omega," which are the first and last letters of the Greek alphabet (A and Ω), we understand what he means. He's saying that Jesus encompasses all history and the entire physical and spiritual universe.

This mystical reverence for the alphabet, combined with the status of Greek as the international language of the Mediterranean and the Near East at the time of Jesus, may help explain why the rabbis at the Council of Jamnia decided to bring Daniel into the canon. As I explained, the Hebrew Bible as originally conceived had 23 books; that's 22 + 1, which you can think of as symbolizing the perfection of the Hebrew alphabet and then some. But that structure was conceived before Alexander the Great made Greek the international language.

By the time of the Council of Jamnia, however, Greek was well established, and a majority of the world's Jews was probably more fluent in Greek than in Hebrew or even Aramaic. Greek has 24 letters. Is it possible the rabbis had that in mind when, with Daniel, they bumped the total for the canon up to 24? I think it's possible, though we can't prove it, since we don't have the conference minutes.

Did the Dead Sea Scrolls reveal anything lacking in the canonical version of the Hebrew Bible?

Yes. The book of Samuel is probably the most dramatic example. The Dead Sea Scrolls have helped us to correct a number of scribal errors and restore omissions from Samuel. A dramatic example can be found at the end of 1 Samuel 10, where an entire paragraph had been omitted from the standard Masoretic Text. The restored paragraph, about a foreign king who had a bad habit of gouging out the Israelites' eyes, doesn't change our theology, or what the Bible is about. But it helps us to have as complete as possible a picture. It's all about getting to the oldest copy of the Bible. If we could find the author's autographs rather than a scribe's signature, their original manuscripts, then, in theory, we could get at the undiluted Word of God.

In the nineteenth century, scholars valued the Septuagint more than the Masoretic Text. Then there was a reaction against the Septuagint in favor of the Masoretic Text. This is how the pendulum swings in biblical studies, as it does in every field. Now we realize the Septuagint and the Masoretic Text are simply two different manuscripts — sometimes one is better, sometimes the other. The Greek represents and translates a Hebrew text that is different from our standard Masoretic Text. This should instill in us a certain humility.

Historical reality is always more complex and fascinating than the orthodox of any tradition would like us to believe. The winners rewrite history, and the rewrite is almost always a simplification. Simplifications are helpful to give us an initial grasp, but we should never content ourselves with them.

Do We Have the Wrong Hebrew Bible?
A Primer on Source Criticism

Thanks to the Dead Sea Scrolls, can we finally restore the original Hebrew Bible?

Pretty much, although for some books like Samuel and Jeremiah the evidence is better than for others. We will never reach perfection, but we're in a better position now to reconstruct the original manuscript. We're in control.

Will the study of the Dead Sea Scrolls lead to a more accurate, more intelligible Old Testament in its pre-Christian state?

All the Dead Sea Scrolls are pre-Christian, so they have already contributed to more accurate study, providing important context and commentary. Overall, we have processed a lot of new information.

The Scrolls have been especially helpful in helping us reconstruct original texts. The fact is, we don't have a single autograph, or original manuscript, of any of the books in the Bible. Instead, we have copies of copies. Over centuries of copying, variations develop and accidents occur, far more incidental than deliberate. In the last chapter, you recall, we talked about haplography, dittography, and other scribal errors. And once in a while, a scribe does us a favor by improving the spelling.

But those autographs must have existed at some point, and it's the job of the biblical scholars to reconstruct them, to recreate them with their best research and best guesses.

How do scholars reconstruct a text?

It's a long process. First we use the best manuscripts we have to try to determine the content of the autograph. Throughout this book we've been comparing the Septuagint to the Masoretic Text, and from that you can begin to get an idea of what this entails: going back and forth, examining both texts in close detail, and so forth. We rely on other things as well to help us make decisions: translations, different versions of the manuscripts, and always an underlying assumption that the language is supposed to make sense and convey meaningful points. All these help us look for clues.

Sometimes we get stuck. When that happens, there's the possibility of emendation — that is, changing or correcting the manuscripts we're working with, based on the guess that a mistake was made somewhere along the line. Most of the time, scholars shouldn't do this, but in cases of desperation, speculation is always permissible. Even if an emendation is questionable, it may shed light on how to read, interpret, and understand the book, and it may even provide a new interpretation and thus prove useful.

If a passage remains opaque, it's often because of words whose meanings are lost. Languages related to ancient Hebrew, like Arabic and Syriac, sometimes help with difficult words, but they can only go so far. In the end, we're not going to solve everything, but attempting to do so is a good idea. Even when we're convinced we're wrong, a speculation still offers hope.

If an artifact is a fake, can we still learn something useful from it?

You might remember the now-infamous "James Ossuary" whose discovery was announced in 2002. It bears an Aramaic inscription, "Ya'akov bar Yosef akhui diYeshua" ("James, the son of Joseph, the brother of Jesus"). At first it was hailed as archaeological proof of Jesus' existence; soon it came to be seen as a forgery. However, even if it is a fake, it has stirred up a lot of interest and a careful study of the language of burial inscriptions. All this is very helpful.

Two favorite mantras of mine are "Be skeptical," which you have to be if you're a scholar, and "Be especially skeptical of the skeptics," because skepticism is too easy a position to assume. If someone routinely says of every new discovery, "It's a fake," then they dismiss it and it's over for them. They never have to change their minds or consider new ideas. The fact is, every new discovery may open a door we didn't even know was there.

I'll tell you something about spotting fakes, though. The fact that we have found something we haven't seen before or don't understand doesn't necessarily indicate a forgery. On the contrary, if it's a fake, we would expect it to conform very precisely to authentic material that has already been found. Otherwise it wouldn't convince anyone. Who would take a chance like that? And the argument that fakes turn out to be clumsy is self-defeating, because that would mean that a fake attempts to be exposed, when it actually intends to elude detection.

I've heard about the Documentary Hypothesis. Can you tell us about that? Does it help us reconstruct the original text of the Hebrew Bible?

The Documentary Hypothesis is the idea that underlying the Bible, particularly the Pentateuch, as we have it today are earlier, separate documents, each of which was originally composed to stand alone.

We do not have any copies of these supposed original works anymore. But postulating that they existed helps us to answer a number of questions about the Pentateuch. For example, why are there various writing styles? And why are different names for God used in different places? And why is there repitition and duplication of certain details? All these things can be explained if we assume that the Pentateuch as we have it now is a result of editing together several different documents.

Julius Wellhausen, the great German scholar of the late nineteenth and early twentieth centuries, is the one who formulated the Documentary Hypothesis. He argued persuasively, building on the work of earlier German scholars, that multiple strands of tradition had been woven together to produce the Torah. In other words, the Pentateuch was not written by one person. (According to tradition, Moses had been that one person.) Wellhausen saw the Torah as the product of a series of editors who had combined four major literary sources, which scholars call J (the Yahwist source), E (the Elohist source), P (the Priestly source), and D (the Deuteronomic source).

Will you give us descriptions of J, E, D, and P?

J and E are usually considered to be the two oldest sources. J gets its name from the fact that it uses the name Yahweh (in

German, *Jahweh*) for God. In the classic analysis, J was probably written in the tenth or ninth century B.C., that is, around the time of King David and King Solomon. J is our major source for the book of Genesis. It takes a primary interest in the events and places of the southern part of the Holy Land, what was the Kingdom of Judah in the time of the divided monarchy. (You can remember this by recalling that "J" also stands for Judah and Jerusalem.)

E uses a different name for God, Elohim, and would be the next-oldest source, dating from the ninth or eighth century B.C. E is responsible for parts of Genesis, and much of the books of Exodus and Numbers. In contrast to J, E is concerned with the northern Kingdom of Israel. I should tell you, though, that E's very existence has always been in question. In the process of editing that I mentioned earlier, much more of E was cut than of J. The first story we have from E is found in Genesis 20, the story of Abraham and Sarah and King Abimelech. It's hard to believe that a narrative history of Israel, which is what E (like J) was supposed to have been, would have left out all the earlier incidents that are so familiar to us from J. This has led some scholars to think that E never existed as a complete, independent source.

D is our source for almost all of the book of Deuteronomy, and probably Joshua, Judges, Samuel, and Kings as well. It's a big debate among scholars whether D preceded P or P preceded D. The tendency today is to put D somewhat earlier — as early as the eighth or seventh century B.C., connected with King Hezekiah rather than King Josiah. The classic dating of the sources hinged on the idea that Josiah's reformation, which is described at some length in 2 Kings 23, was inspired by the discovery of a manuscript scholars name D — essentially the book of Deuteronomy — in the eighteenth year of Josiah's reign, which we can date to around 622 B.C. The question is whether Deuteronomy was written specifically to be "discovered" at that time, or whether it had already existed and the discovery was genuine. In other words, was it a plant or was it a surprise?

Finally, P, the Priestly source, provides genealogies and information about the priesthood and worship, and it contributes the first chapter of Genesis and the book of Leviticus. Wellhausen argued that P was the latest source, added to all the others after 539 B.C. But many scholars today are arguing the other way, saying that P contains preexilic material and a form of classic, preexilic Hebrew. So it's still an open question whether the order is J, E, D, P or J, E, P, D.

That's a very basic analysis of the primary narrative of the Hebrew Bible according to the Documentary Hypothesis. The result is the Torah in its final form, as we have it today.

Can you say a little more about King Josiah's connection to the D source?

Scholars often associate Deuteronomy with the book found by King Josiah's high priest, Hilkiah, in 622 B.C. You can read the story in 2 Kings 22-23: the king ordered some repairs to be made to the Temple in Jerusalem, and in the course of those repairs, a long-lost scroll was found containing "the book of the law" — the book of Deuteronomy. After hearing the scroll read to him, Josiah tore his clothes. He realized that the people of Israel had not been keeping God's law properly, and so he promptly instituted wide-ranging religious reforms.

That's the story as we have it, but scholarly skepticism proposes that the scroll Hilkiah found wasn't long-lost at all, but rather written and then planted to be found. The idea is that the priests wanted to implement reform, and "finding" an "ancient" scroll would give them an excuse to do so. This skepticism is based on Deuteronomy's style and vocabulary: the language of the book is late Hebrew, not the Hebrew of Moses' day.

On the other hand, it would be pretty risky to try to fool the king! If the scroll were a hoax, we can imagine him asking such indelicate questions as, "Why is the ink still wet?"

More recently the idea has gained favor that Deuteronomy goes back just a century or so before Josiah, to King Hezekiah's time. The language, grammar, and other characteristics of Deuteronomy all fit with this period. But this is just the latest theory; we'll probably never know exactly what happened that day in the Temple. In any event, none of the Pentateuch is written in the Hebrew of Moses' time, not even the "early" sources, J and E. But we can still distinguish classic, preexilic Hebrew prose and poetry, in which most of the Pentateuch is written, from later forms of the language.

Can you help us solve the JEDP/JEPD controversy?

Well, I mentioned earlier that Julius Wellhausen, the great German scholar who is generally credited with the classic statement of the Documentary Hypothesis, argued that the order is J, E, D, P. In this view, P is the latest source, and priestly editors put the Torah in its final form sometime after 539 B.C. Today scholars argue with Wellhausen and with one another about whether D or P was added last. But they agree that the general approach of the Documentary Hypothesis is the best explanation for the differences in terminology, theology, and geographic and historic interests in various parts of the Torah.

My private solution to the dilemma doesn't appeal to anyone except me because it's too obvious, and that stupefies scholars. Since P and D have very different vocabularies, styles, and points of view, and show no influence of one upon the other, I say P and D are contemporary, written at the same time. Roughly speaking, P is oriented to the south, and D is oriented to the north, like J and E, for which a very similar argument can be made; namely, that neither J nor E show any influence of one on the other, and the division between north and south makes sense. One clue is that the name "Sinai" is associated with J and P, whereas "Horeb," the holy mountain's other name, is associated with E and D. This seems to conform to a cultural and linguistic division between north and south. So, J and P in the south, E and D in the north. Why not?

Surreal Theologians:
Belief and Practice at Qumrân

If we had discovered the Scrolls before 1947, would Judaism be different?

It's very doubtful. No matter when the Scrolls were discovered, their discovery would not have been likely to change the course of an entire religion. You'll recall that the canon of the Hebrew Bible was fixed by the rabbis at the Council of Jamnia in A.D. 92, so we wouldn't expect any major changes after that. After the destruction of the Temple in A.D. 70, the priesthood was effectively abolished and the rabbis defined Judaism as it is today.

Besides, even in their day, the Essenes didn't represent the mainstream of Jewish belief and practice. They were just one of four main groups in Judaism; the others were the Pharisees, the Sadducees, and the Zealots or revolutionaries. In its earliest days, Christianity was considered a sect of Judaism as well.

How did the Pharisees, Sadducees, and Zealots differ from the Essenes?

As you might expect, there were both similarities and differences. The Essenes had a certain kinship with the Pharisees, because both movements had their origin in the Hasidic movement of the Maccabean age. The Maccabees, you remember, were the ones who rebelled against Syria and against Greek cultural influences in the 160s B.C. The Hasidim were those devout Jews who insisted on living according to the Law of Moses as enshrined in the Torah. So both the Pharisees and the Essenes were concerned with keeping the religious law, although they did so in very different ways. You might recall that the New Testament paints the Pharisees as some of Jesus' chief opponents. And St. Paul was a Pharisee before his conversion to Christianity.

The Sadducees were like the Essenes in that both groups had a high degree of reverence for the priesthood. But unlike the Essenes, the Sadducees weren't waiting for the end of the world. The Essenes were very apocalyptically-minded, but the Sadducees had a much more secular mindset. The first-century historian Josephus describes them as being wealthy, powerful, and argumentative.

The Zealots were concerned with the apocalypse, like the Essenes were. But being extreme nationalists, they expected political revolution to usher it in. Rather than escape the world to wait for the end to come, the Zealots wanted to bring it about with violence.

Which branch of Judaism is closest to the Essenes today?

None is close enough to make such a comparison meaningful. Of the four groups of Jews listed by Josephus — Pharisees, Sadducees, Essenes, and Zealots — only the Pharisees had a future. The usual theory is that Pharisees gradually evolved into what we know as Rabbinic Judaism, which is represented today by three main branches: the Orthodox, Conservative, and Reform movements. But even the Pharisees of first-century Judea did not have a lot in common with the Essenes, apart from their scrupulousness about the law. How much less, then, do the successors of the Pharisees thousands of years later have in common with the Essenes!

What do the Qumrânites call themselves? Can we be sure they were Essenes?

Although we've been using the term throughout this book, the Qumrânites never explicitly call themselves Essenes. We get the term from Josephus, the first-century Jewish historian, who calls them *Essēnoi* or *Essaioi* — the terms most understandable to outsiders. These terms are most likely Greek corruptions of the Hebrew *'ôśê hattôrāh,* "doers of the Law," a description that certainly fits the Qumrân community's conception of itself.

Another proposal is that "Essene" is the Aramaic form of *Hasidim,* "pious ones," which would also apply to the Qumrân community. Ultimately, however, the origin of the name "Essene" is a mystery. We don't know exactly what it means or why it's used.

The Qumrânites referred to themselves with names like "the Children of Light" and "the People of the Covenant." Their idea of "the covenant" is reflected in the fact that there was a two-year initiation process for anyone who wanted to join their community.

Why the two-year trial period for initiates?

The two-year trial period was a time when novices could be scrutinized and their faith, obedience, and repentance clearly proven. Full membership in the Qumrân community required an oath, the acceptance of covenant obligations, and baptism. (The last only for those who repented from wickedness. The penitent had to be purified before coming into contact with the holy members of the inner circle.) Novices were drawn closer into the communal life after one year, but the final step was admission to the common meal, called the "Banquet of the Many," or the "Purity."

A Scroll describes what happened when a novice passed the test: "According to the word of the Many, if the decision favors him to enter the community, they will inscribe him in the order of his rank among his brothers in what concerns the Law, equity, the Purity, and the mingling of his property. His counsel and his judgment shall be for the community." He was then a member for life, with all the benefits and responsibilities that entailed.

The Essenes weren't the only ones with high standards and elaborate obligations, though. Throughout the Bible, oaths and covenants are serious business. And today, many religious orders have similar periods of discernment and initiation — some even longer than two years. Indeed, even joining a church or synagogue today in most cases requires you to take a class. The people who are already part of the community want to make sure you know what you're getting into and really want to go ahead with it.

What was the political structure of the Qumrân community?

The Essenes expected that in the Messianic Age they would be governed by a prophet, a priest, and a king. But until these messianic figures arrived, they followed a Teacher of Righteousness, a religious leader who partially embodied all three of the end-time figures. There also seems to have been a secular leader alongside this religious leader, although it's not clear from the Scrolls just what kind of a role he played. Most likely his role was fiscal, overseeing the community's finances (a task crucial to any religious organization, no matter how ascetic it might be!).

The community employed a political structure that it traced back to the forty years Israel spent wandering in the wilderness: priests, Levites, and laypeople divided into groups called Thousands, Hundreds, Fifties, and Tens — names that were more symbolic than factual, considering that only about 200 Essenes lived at Qumrân. The government was hierarchical, with the Teacher of Righteousness, a Zadokite priest, as the civil authority. (You'll remember from our earlier conversation how important it was to the Essenes at Qumrân to have a *Zadokite* priest as their leader; see p. 50.) In this sense we could describe the political structure at Qumrân as a "priestly theocracy."

Members had a voice in what transpired, much like in a monastic community today, but once a decision was made, there was no room for dissent; total submission was required. Here's a quote from one of the Scrolls regarding community life: "They shall depart from no counsel of the Law to walk in all the stubbornness of their hearts, but they shall be governed by the primitive precepts in which the men of the community were first instructed, until the coming of a prophet and the Messiahs of Aaron and Israel."

Members were arranged by rank, based upon their proven spiritual worthiness, with titles like the Priest, the heads of the sons of Aaron, the Messiah of Israel, the chiefs of the tribes of Israel, and the elders. We don't really know to whom, if anyone, these titles actually referred, but we do know that there was a ranking according to spiritual maturity. Those who had "greater" intelligence, deeds, spirits, morals, and perfect conduct were advanced, while those whose spirits and deeds were petty or selfish became "lesser." And in the assembly, those of higher rank got to speak first.

Was there a law court at Qumrân?

The Damascus Document explains proper behavior for resolving disputes. In a disagreement, the offender should first be approached with witnesses, and if necessary, he could then be brought before the Many. Accusations were never to be made in anger or for revenge. The Overseer would hear the case, but he would pronounce a sentence only if the witnesses were credible and gave their testimony on the day of the incident. As punishment, the offender was excluded from the common meal, the "Purity."

Did a dispute over a calendar cause the Essenes to leave Jerusalem?

We don't really know what caused the Essenes of Qumrân to forsake the Holy City. It was probably a combination of many disagreements, including those over the calendar. What we do know is that while they were in the desert, they devoted a lot of attention to the keeping of holy days according to their sectarian calendar, which was entirely solar — that is, set up so as to match the yearly movement of the sun as closely as possible.

This was a major departure from the mainstream Jewish calendar, which was "lunisolar," or a mixed calendar with both lunar and solar elements. It was "lunar" in that each observed month began with the new moon, but "solar" to the extent that every couple of years an extra month would be thrown in to bring the sequence of months back into alignment with the solar year.

The problem with a purely lunar calendar is that twelve lunar months equals about 354 days, more than ten days short of a solar year. In a purely lunar calendar, such as the Muslim calendar, the months keep slipping back relative to the seasons. After about fifteen or sixteen years, a month that came in the summer would come in the winter, and vice-versa.

Major Jewish religious festivals were agricultural in origin, so variations in the calendar year were unacceptable. Passover had to be celebrated in the spring, so to keep the month of Nisan from slipping too far behind the Spring Equinox, leap-months were added, at first ad hoc and then later according to an established schedule.

To the Qumrânites, however, this was too messy and unacceptable. Their system was much tidier, and they believed it reflected the original order and symmetry of God's creation more faithfully. Their year consisted of 12 months of 30 days each, with an extra transitional day thrown in after every third month. This yielded a year of 364 days, or exactly 52 weeks.

One orderly result of this was that specific dates fell on the same day of the week every year; for example, Passover always started on a Tuesday evening. These dates had a cosmic significance; a festival had to be held on the correct date, or it was even worse than worthless — it was sinful. And since the mainstream Jewish calendar was wrong, the religious establishment at the Temple was breaking God's law all the time.

The problem with neatly-packaged theories, however, is that they seldom fit into reality. We know this had to be the case with the sectarian calendar at Qumrân, since every schoolchild now knows that the solar year is slightly longer than 365 days, hence our solution of the leap year every four years. The 364-day calendar would have led to slippage relative to the seasons — much slower slippage than a purely lunar calendar, but slippage all the same.

We don't know how, if at all, the Qumrân community dealt with this problem. They may have inserted a day periodically, but if they did, no record of it remains in the Scrolls.

What we do have are several documents that plot the interrelationships between phases of the moon, days of the month (according to the Qumrân calendar), religious festivals (some of which are unique to Qumrân), and the terms of duty of the 24 different teams of priests that are mentioned in the books of Chronicles. Since the Qumrân calendar itself seems to have dispensed with the moon as a marker of time, it's not clear why the phases of the moon remained important, unless it was purely for astronomical purposes.

Did the Essenes perform animal sacrifice?

That's an important question. This was a group of Jews who believed that the Temple had been corrupted and was therefore unusable. They thought that after the great, apocalyptic war of the end time, they would return to Jerusalem and cleanse the Temple, just as the Maccabees had done after expelling the Syrians in 164 B.C. But meanwhile, what did they do for Passover?

The answer is that, yes, they prepared their own sacrifices, since they couldn't and wouldn't go to the Temple. And this wasn't a problem for them, since they reasoned that Moses and the Israelites had sacrificed for 40 years in the desert without a Temple.

According to Josephus, the Essenes sent gifts to the Temple, but they did not offer sacrifices there because of their different concepts of purity. Instead, they practiced sacrifices independently, outside of the Temple. The Essenes believed that the only prerequisite for making a sacrifice was to obey God's laws, and their obedience made their sacrifices at Qumrân acceptable, despite the prohibitions in Deuteronomy 12 against offering animal sacrifice anywhere but "at the place where the LORD will choose to set his name," which was the Deuteronomist's code for Jerusalem.

The Temple Scroll regulates the sacrifices of goats, rams, oxen, lambs, and sheep and once refers to eating the firstborn of the flock once a year in a chosen place. On the Day of Atonement, Yom Kippur, a burning of whole animals would be performed: "one bull, one ram, seven male lambs a year old, one male goat for a sin offering, besides the sin offering for expiation and their cereal (grain) offering and their libation according to the regulation for the bull, the ram, the lambs, and the goat."

Interestingly, in some open areas of the settlement, the excavators found bones of sheep, cattle, and goats meticulously buried in jars. These were the bones of animals eaten in sacred meals.

Did the Essenes believe in fate or in free will? How did they think they earned their salvation?

Like Christians and Jews today, they found a loophole. Or, to put it another way, they grasped the paradox with both hands. The Scrolls express both God's election and humanity's obligation to respond: "Who is like Your people, Israel, which You have chosen for Yourself from all the peoples of the lands, a people of holy ones of the Covenant, schooled in Your law and learned in insight, who hearken to the voice of the Honored One?" In other words, everything that is going to happen has already been decided by God, but human beings are responsible for their own education, discipline, reasoning, and behaviors.

To earn their salvation, the Essenes believed they had to lead a disciplined life, curbing their natural impulses and appetites, which they viewed as negative. They also had to have solidarity as a group. Very practically speaking, without everyone pitching in and cooperating, their community in the wilderness couldn't survive. And always they had to keep the outside world, the "Children of Darkness," from contaminating them. There was a vast separation between insiders and outsiders: you must love those inside, and avoid contact with those outside.

Did the Essenes feel as though they were bringing heaven to earth, following a model of heavenly activity?

They may not have felt that heaven was literally descending, but they felt an obligation to pattern earthly existence after the heavenly model, doing things on earth as closely as possible to the way they were done in heaven. This is why their calendar was so important to them. The festivals that God decreed in his Torah weren't only for humanity. They were for the angels and the entire universe. The Sabbath was observed in heaven as it was on earth.

True worship always has had a cosmic dimension. Even the tabernacle in the Torah, which was a portable tent, served as a model of the actual palace that God was thought to inhabit in heaven.

Did the Essenes believe people were evil and that God alone is good?

It's quite striking that the Essenes' view of human errancy is closer to early Christianity's view than it is to mainstream Judaism's, although there are certainly differences. The Pharisees seemed to think that people had a good tendency and an evil tendency, and that humans are essentially free to make their own decisions regarding which of the two to follow. On the other hand, the Essenes as well as early Christians viewed human beings as somehow being fundamentally disposed toward evil, so that it takes great effort and various techniques to move to the right side.

Were they elitist?

The Essenes weren't worried about drawing big numbers of members. They didn't believe in "church growth" and certainly weren't "seeker sensitive." Their rules were strict and the requirements for membership weeded out those who couldn't conform or contribute to the Community. Not only did the Essenes feel more pure and true to the Covenant than other Jews, but as men they felt superior to women. So yes, they were very exclusive. They didn't want to let the wrong people in.

Do you think the Essenes were celibate?

I believe that as the "community of God," the men of Qumrân did remain celibate, because they would not follow "the order of the earth" and marry. In the cemetery at Qumrân, only men's bones were found. By contrast, at the adjacent community of Ein Feshkha, also thought to be made up of Essenes, bones of women and children were found, so it looks as though Josephus was right and that there were two settlements. The Qumrân community seems to have been entirely male and celibate, while Ein Feshkha was mixed.

The easiest way out of the discrepancy is to recognize two groups — as Josephus does — that were quite similar: two orders, one of celibate priests, the other of family-oriented laypeople who marry.

What was the Essenes' ritual meal like?

At Qumrân, having a common meal was everyday practice at midday and in the evening. Josephus observed that the Essenes went to a meal "as to some holy precinct." They bathed first, and only initiates were allowed to take a seat. The order of the meal was carefully prescribed.

The wine and bread were blessed whenever as many as ten men were solemnly gathered together. A Scroll prescribes the protocol: "Wherever there are ten men, there shall not lack one who studies the Law continually, day and night, concerning the conduct of one with another. And the Many shall keep vigil in common for a third of every night in the year, to read the Book, to study the Law, and to bless in common." Along with prayers, a lector read Scripture at each meal.

We can find parallels with the Essenes' ritual meals in both Jewish Shabbat dinners and the Christian sacrament of the Lord's Supper or Eucharist. All three meals have retrospective and prospective elements: looking back to the founding of a community, while looking forward to an event at the end of time.

What about their ritual baths?

Water washes away dirt, but the action of washing is also symbolically important. As with all of the Essenes' codes for cultic purity, the demands are strict and highly regulated. At Qumrân, baptism was almost certainly immersion in *running* water as a sign that a man had taken covenant obligations upon himself. But baptism was not intrinsically effective; a man had to be repentant, obedient, and faithful, or even "seas or rivers" couldn't make him pure.

Was John the Baptist an Essene?

That's certainly an idea that is entertained, although it has never been the majority opinion among scholars. Even since the Dead Sea Scrolls were found, this has never been the pre-

One of several ritual baths (mikva´ot) at Qumrân, used for purposes of purification by immersion in the initiation of members and repeatedly for cultic cleansing.   (Jodi Magness)

dominant view. There are striking similarities between the Essenes and John the Baptist — even more than between the Essenes and Jesus.

For example, John is said to have grown up in the wilderness, and how do you grow up in the wilderness without being a part of a community? The Essenes were in the desert. Both the Essenes and John were expecting the coming of the Messiah; and both placed high importance on the ritual of bap-

John and Jesus were contemporaries of the Essenes, but they baptized in public, calling all people (Jews and Gentiles) to salvation. The Essenes only baptized their own members.

tism. But even if John was once a member of the Essenes, he seems to have broken away from them.

Could the Scrolls be the remains of the library of the Temple in Jerusalem?

What seems certain is that some of the Scrolls were not written in Qumrân but were brought by the Essenes when they fled to the wilderness. These documents predate the settlement in Qumrân, which didn't begin until 150 B.C.

According to paleographic analysis and carbon-14 testing, some of the Scrolls date to the early third or second centuries B.C. In other words, the Scrolls were already in existence before the Qumrân settlement and were no doubt brought by the people from Jerusalem.

If the older Scrolls did in fact originate at the Temple, did the Essenes steal them?

If the Scrolls were taken from the official collection in the Temple, you might call it "stealing." But it's very hard to tell where they came from. They may have been privately owned, or they might have been part of the library collection connected with the priesthood. Besides, the Essenes, or at least a number of them, were authentic priests. They would therefore have some legitimate claim to the manuscripts, so there is no reason to accuse them of stealing.

The Dead Sea Scrolls, the New Testament, and Early Christianity

Did early Christian communities have the same priestly structure as the Essene community at Qumrân?

No, they didn't. Early Christianity was a movement of laypeople. Jewish priests certainly could have become Christians, but once they did, they wouldn't automatically have any special privileges or any particular role to play. Matthew, one of the twelve disciples, might have been a Levite; but not one apostle is called a priest in the Jewish sense.

Why are the Essenes never mentioned in the New Testament, unlike the Pharisees, Sadducees, and the followers of John the Baptist?

That remains a mystery. There were Essene groups (called "conventicles") in the cities, probably numbering more members than at Qumrân, so it wouldn't be unreasonable to think that Jesus interacted with some of them. On the other hand, the people who lived at Qumrân were hermits, so we would expect them to be almost invisible to their contemporaries.

What kinds of parallels have scholars discovered between the New Testament and the Dead Sea Scrolls?

We compare everything, and we do find parallels in such things as theological language, ritual procedures, and a shared apocalyptic framework. We have traced specific passages in which a concept like the "Children of Light" and the "Children of Darkness" from the Dead Sea Scrolls is echoed in the New Testament, especially in the book of Revelation, which has many similarities with Essene writings. The centerpiece of Revelation is the last war, Armageddon, which resonates with the Essenes' description of the imminent final battle between forces of good and evil.

However, it takes complex reasoning to see the Christian movement in Qumrân. The Essenes are closer to the tradition of the Hebrew Bible than they are to that of the New Testament.

What is the most striking parallel?

Echoes of the Dead Sea Scrolls occur throughout the New Testament, but especially in the writings of Paul and John. Paul expected the end soon and described the sequence in 1 Corinthians. The basic chronology of the last days is quite similar in the Dead Sea Scrolls, although some of the specifics differ. Based on their reading of Scripture, the Essenes pictured three eschatological figures who would appear before a culminating battle between the forces of good and the forces of evil: a Davidic king, a future high priest, and an eschatological prophet. In the New Testament, these same figures were expected, but they were seen as fulfilled in the person of Jesus. The Essenes, however, lacked a concept of the resurrection. When the Teacher of Righteousness died, he died; if he was going to be raised again, it would be at the end with everyone else.

Are there parallels between the Gospel According to John and the Dead Sea Scrolls?

More than any other Gospel, the book of John shows connections with the Dead Sea Scrolls. Both John and the Dead Sea Scrolls are products of sectarian Judaism, emphasizing the unity of the community and the stance of "us versus them." "We" are inside and the rest are outside, including Gentiles and most Jews.

There is similar imagery, too. Both John and the Scrolls show interest in being on the side of "light" rather than "darkness." And the Essenes write of the "Spirit of Truth," which has some similarities with the Holy Spirit as described in John.

Was Paul borrowing language from the Dead Sea Scrolls when he contrasted "righteousness and lawlessness," "light and darkness," and "Christ and Belial" (2 Corinthians 6:14-15)?

The scholarly consensus is that Paul used several terms typical of the Essenes. The most striking example is Paul's reference to Belial (*Beliar* in Greek), a demon popular in Jewish mythology and frequently mentioned in the Dead Sea Scrolls.

Altogether, Paul uses six keywords in 2 Corinthians 6:14-15 that don't appear anywhere else in his writing. This led one scholar, Pierre Benoit, to call the passage "a meteor fallen from the heaven of Qumrân into Paul's epistle." So there is suspicion that Paul may have been more familiar with the Essenes than is usually thought, and that he may have actually studied their material. His education was quite comprehensive.

Would it be accurate to say that the Dead Sea Scrolls have revolutionized the study of the New Testament?

I would tend to say that the Scrolls provide a more balanced, scholarly approach to biblical studies rather than a revolutionary one. One major debate in New Testament studies that the Scrolls have shed light on is whether the author of the Gospel of John was rooted in the Jewish philosophical tradition or whether he owed more to Greek thought. The Scrolls show that in every case, the language of John's gospel and epistles, although it is Greek, nevertheless translates Hebrew and Aramaic terms that turn up in the Dead Sea Scrolls. Therefore, John is more Jewish than Greek.

But trying too hard to relate the Essenes to Christianity is not germane because as far as we can tell, there was no direct contact between the community at Qumrân and the followers of Jesus.

Where did the Essenes get the idea that three figures would usher in the end?

According to the Scrolls, the final battle would start when three leaders appeared in a very specific order. The triumvirate would consist of the prophet, priest, and king I mentioned earlier. The prophet's role is to identify the two other figures, so he would come first, and the other two soon after. The idea comes from the tradition of Samuel who, as a prophet, anointed the king (a high priest already being in office). Another example of this template is David as king, Nathan as prophet, and Zadok as high priest.

Could Jesus have been the messianic prophet the Essenes were expecting?

No. The Essenes would have expected their prophet to point in turn to a priest and a king, and Jesus didn't do that. The early Christians got around this issue by claiming that Jesus filled all three roles himself, but the Essenes were anticipating three separate individuals. Jesus alone wouldn't have cut it for them.

Jesus did have one characteristic in common with the Essenes' messianic prophet. He performed miracles. The classic prophets — Moses, Elijah, Elisha, even Samuel — all demonstrated their commission by performing miracles: Moses parted the Red Sea by raising his rod, Samuel helped defeat the Philistines, Elijah defeated the prophets of Baal, and Elisha raised the dead. Only prophets do these things. It's worth noting that neither John the Baptist nor the Teacher of Righteousness at Qumrân are recorded as performing any miracles, so they would have been automatically disqualified in the Essenes' eyes. Because of his miracles, Jesus might have come a little closer, but not close enough for the Essenes.

Interestingly, the New Testament writers downplayed Jesus' role as a prophet as well. If Jesus had been a prophet, the implication would be that there was someone greater coming after him, and for the Christians, there wasn't. To them, Jesus was the fulfillment of prophecy, not a forerunner. So they transferred the prophetic role to John the Baptist.

Could Jesus have been the Essenes' long-awaited messianic priest?

Again, no. According to the Synoptic Gospels, Jesus is descended from David, who was from the tribe of Judah. That's the wrong lineage to qualify as a priest. The messianic priest, like all true priests in the Essenes' eyes, was to be a descendant of Zadok, a priest in the line of Aaron. That's a totally different bloodline.

Also, Jewish law makes it difficult for the same person to be both priest and king, so even a figure as charismatic as Jesus did not really stand a chance to fill all three roles in the popular mind. The Maccabees are the classic example of people who tried to be both kings and high priests, but they ultimately failed at both. The Romans took care of that.

The early Christians saw Jesus as a priest by reinterpreting and reinventing the priestly role, assigning it to Jesus alone. The New Testament book of Hebrews makes the argument that Jesus is the new, eternal high priest.

By the way, the words for "priest" in the Old Testament and the New are very different. The word in the New Testament actually comes from the Greek *presbyteros,* "presbyter" or "elder." It has nothing to do with the Hebrew Bible's Levitical priesthood, whose members were *kohanim* in Hebrew. Peter, James, and other leaders of the church were "priests" only in the sense of being "elders." As far as we know, they were not Levites, and almost certainly not "priests" in the Old Testament sense.

Could Jesus have been the messianic king that the Essenes expected?

No, he couldn't have been their king, either. In the first century A.D., popular expectation among the Jewish people focused on a king who would beat the Romans. They wanted a warrior. The Essenes and early Christians downplayed this aspect because these groups didn't do much successful fighting. The Essenes expected direct divine intervention — they were not bellicose.

The Christian tradition made John the Baptist the prophet who identified Jesus as the king, and the Gospel writers provided Jesus with the Davidic lineage necessary for a true king of Israel. (The irony is that 90% of Jewish people at the time could claim to be descendants of David.) But the Essenes expected a high priest to confirm the identity of the messianic king, and that didn't happen to Jesus.

Is there any mention of early Christians or Jesus himself in the Dead Sea Scrolls?

The word "Christian" does not occur anywhere in the Dead Sea Scrolls. Nor is there any mention of Jesus. But you would expect some mention, seeing that the community seems to have come to an end in A.D. 68, when the Romans came into town. Jesus was crucified somewhere between A.D. 29 and 31 at the age of 33. So there were some years of overlap, but the Qumrân community was very isolated in its desert outpost, and it took the Christian movement a little while to make its presence felt. Still, although no evidence of interaction or mutual recognition has yet been found, the possibility that it occurred still exists.

Do *you* think any of the people of Qumrân had ever encountered Jesus, or had at least heard of him?

Like I said, nothing in the Scrolls refers to Jesus. Nevertheless, some scholars think that Jesus may have studied at Qumrân. When the Scrolls were first discovered, G. Lankester Harding, the Director of the Jordanian Department of Antiquities at the time, wrote an article called "Where Christ Himself May Have Studied: An Essene Monastery at Khirbet Qumrân" (1955). After citing other scholars who believed Jesus had studied with the Essenes, Harding waxes rhapsodic about the ruins of Qumrân: "These, then, are the very walls He looked upon, the corridors and rooms through which He wandered and in which He sat, brought to light once again after nearly 1900 years." But are they? I don't know.

Some scholars have also wondered whether there are allusions to the Essenes in the Gospels. Jesus refers explicitly to Pharisees and Sadducees, but never to the Essenes. This could be due to the Essenes' nature as pacifists who had withdrawn into the desert, disappearing from the political scene in Jerusalem. But some scholars wonder if Jesus was making a veiled reference to the celibate Essenes when he praised those who "have made themselves eunuchs for the sake of the kingdom of heaven" (Matthew 19:12). Others claim that Jesus alluded to the community at Qumrân when he said, "So if they say to you, 'Look, he is in the desert,' do not go out" (Matthew 24:24). Here again, reading between the lines offers endless possibilities, but speculation does not make something true.

Could Jesus be a "Teacher of Righteousness" according to the Essenes' definition?

The authoritative teacher described in the Scrolls has similarities with Jesus. Both spoke of good and evil and used the term "Children of Light" to describe those who did God's will (see Luke 16:8). Both were persecuted by the Sadducees, the priestly party, and ultimately condemned to death. Both the Righteous Teacher and Jesus proclaimed judgment on Jerusalem and established communities that expected their prophet's return and judgment of the world.

But there are also huge differences. The followers of the Righteous Teacher at Qumrân viewed him as an interpreter and a teacher of God's law; the followers of Jesus, on the other hand, saw him as the actual Messiah, fulfilling the eschatological prophecies of the Jewish Scriptures.

In the end, speculations about Jesus being an Essene or a Teacher of Righteousness stimulate the imagination, but they shouldn't be confused with certainties. It is very unlikely that Jesus was ever an Essene, and it is therefore impossible for him to have been a Teacher of Righteousness by their standards.

Is anyone close to being a "Righteous Teacher" today?

Well, a lot depends on your perspective. There are certainly people who have played a prophetic role in our society, especially with regard to social issues: Martin Luther King Jr., Mother Teresa, and so on. But that's not the same as the Righteous Teacher, who was considered *the* prophet by his followers at Qumrân.

For parallels to the Righteous Teacher, it's probably better to think in terms of the founders of other religious movements: Moses in Judaism, Jesus in Christianity, Mohammed in Islam, and so forth. If you want to get closer to our own time, the founder of the Bahá'í faith, Bahá'u'lláh (1817-1892), and the founder of Mormonism, Joseph Smith (1805-1844), seem to fulfill similar roles for the religious movements that they started.

The Beginning of the End

Can you tell me how the Essenes read Scripture: as a legal document that legislates conduct; as an allegory that stands for a heavenly reality; as a historical document; or as a prophecy of the end times?

All of the above, but I wouldn't use the categories of law, allegory, history, and prophecy. The Essenes interpreted Scripture above all *as relating to themselves in the present.* The best example of this might be the Habakkuk Commentary that I mentioned earlier (see page 24). In the Commentary, the book of Habakkuk's references to Assyrians and Egyptians were reinterpreted as references to the kingdoms of the Seleucids and Ptolemies, which were contemporary with Qumrân.

Of course, people have been updating the ancient prophecies for as long as the Bible has been around. They take something that originally applied to a specific time and place, and they apply it to later times and places. This happens all the time. People want their own generation to be the generation of fulfillment.

Remember, from the beginning the prophets were interested in something that was going to happen soon, and likewise, so were their successors. It takes considerable ingenuity to adapt ancient sayings to later situations. The Essenes did it beautifully.

The way the Essenes saw it, Scripture contained secret information about a later time. To give an example, the prophet Habakkuk talks about the Babylonians, whom he calls the *kasdîm*, or the Chaldeans, in the sixth century B.C. The Qumrân commentator equates the *kasdîm* with a people he calls the *kittiyyîm*, a generic term for Greeks (probably derived from Kition, a city on Cyprus). So what applied to the Babylonians in Habakkuk's time, now applied to the Seleucids in Syria and the Ptolemies in Egypt, and this became the key for interpreting the prophets.

For the Qumrânites who understood themselves to be "the true Israel," the Hellenizing powers of Syria and Egypt were as much of a threat to their existence as the Babylonians and Assyrians had been to the historical kingdoms of Israel and Judah some 600 to 700 years earlier.

Did Ezekiel foretell the settlement at Qumrân as part of his eschatological timeline?

The Essenes thought so. In Ezekiel 4, the prophet predicts a 390-year period of punishment for the Israelites because of their sins. If we take 586 B.C. as the starting date — the year when the last remnant of David's united Israelite kingdom was destroyed by the Babylonians — then 390 years brings us down to 196 B.C.

But, like I said earlier, I think the Essenes' departure from Jerusalem had to be while Hananiah was high priest, and he was deposed in 170 B.C. (see page 50). So if we take 176 B.C. as a rough guess at the year when the Teacher of Righteousness led the Essenes to settle at Qumrân, then Ezekiel's calculations leave the Essenes about 20 years short.

So they invented a 20-year interval to connect their own exodus to Ezekiel's prophecy. Israel's "punishment" ended in 196 B.C., they thought, in the sense that even though they didn't yet have a leader, they formed a sort of proto-community of "true Israelites" who were dissatisfied with the corruption and laxity of the Jerusalem establishment but didn't yet know quite what to do about it.

The Damascus Document describes a 20-year period during which the Essenes wandered around, lost and leaderless, and this would have been between 196-176 B.C. Yet the germ of their community was formed, and when the Teacher of Righteousness appeared, they finally found someone charismatic enough to articulate their grievances. These are expressed in a Scroll that scholars call 4Q MMT, which not only itemizes the ritual sins of the Temple priesthood, but also basically says, "Since you won't listen, we're out of here!"

I think the Essenes were embarrassed by the 20-year gap between Ezekiel's prophecy and the advent of their Teacher, and that accounts for the "20 years" in the Damascus Document. If you try to ignore that patch and place the Teacher in 196 B.C., you not only leave the time of the man I identify as the Wicked Priest, you also put the Essenes at Qumrân several decades earlier than the archaeological evidence will support. There is no evidence of the Essenes' settlement before 150 B.C.

Getting back to Ezekiel, we have other evidence that the Essenes understood themselves in terms of his prophecy. The site they chose, Qumrân, is precisely where Ezekiel's mighty, healing river would flow into the Dead Sea, turning the salt water into fresh water and inaugurating a new Eden, a heaven on earth, right there at Qumrân. So even though in 176 B.C. it was one of the least promising spots on the face of the planet, they were convinced it had a great future.

Did the people of Qumrân believe in resurrection?

It seems that they expected the righteous to be resurrected all at once at the end of time, as it is described in Daniel 12:1-3.

One thing scholars debate about related to this is how the Essenes viewed the body and soul as interconnected. The ancient historian Hippolytus writes that the Essenes believed in a final judgment at which the bodies of the righteous would rise to be reunited with their souls, which in the meantime awaited the final judgment in a "luminous realm." The War Scroll mentions "those who will rise from the earth," and one of the Thanksgiving Psalms claims that "those who lie in the dust have raised a flagstaff" and defeated the wicked. But are these references to the dead being literally resurrected, or are they metaphors? Some scholars think that the Essenes believed in an immortal body, while others think they believed only in an immortal soul.

Scholars do agree, though, that the Scrolls don't specify what exactly would happen to the unrighteous. There is no eternal hellfire mentioned in the Scrolls.

Since the Essenes didn't expect universal salvation, did they want all the wicked people (defined as everyone outside their Essene fold) to be wiped out so they alone could reign with God?

The Essenes didn't hope for a messiah who would convert the wicked and thus save the whole earth. In a 40-year war, the Children of Light — the Essenes teaming up with God and the angels Michael, Raphael, and Sariel — would totally defeat the Children of Darkness, who would be led by the demon Belial. The War Scroll gives army formations and battle plans, lists the necessary military equipment, and gives specific prayers and battle cries for the High Priest. In the absence of a kingly Messiah, the High Priest acts as Commander-in-Chief.

After a thanksgiving ceremony, a great and final battle against the *Kittim* or *Kittiyyim* (the Gentiles) ends history. The War Scroll also describes the bloody aftermath with glee, celebrating the certain defeat of the Children of Darkness. The whole event was scripted with great optimism.

The Scrolls mention many figures, both good and bad, by titles rather than proper names; for example, "False Oracle," "Lion of Wrath," "Lamb," "Righteous Teacher." Are these recurring prototypes, or do they refer to specific, unique individuals?

In most cases, these labels apply to specific people whom the Essenes expected at the dawn of what they called the "New Age." In several cases, I think we can identify the person. For example, the Lion of Wrath was the Sadducee Alexander Jannaeus, who opposed the Pharisees as the belligerent priest-king of Judea from 103-76 B.C. Josephus describes his cruelty: "He did a thing that was as cruel as could be. While he feasted with his concubines in a conspicuous place, he ordered some 800 of the Jews to be crucified, and slaughtered their children and wives before the eyes of the still living wretches." It is no surprise that in the Talmud — the rabbinic book of commentary on the law — Alexander Jannaeus also appears as a wicked tyrant.

I think the Essenes knew exactly who they meant by each label, and they didn't use real names because they feared retaliation. Ambiguity is a strategy for self-preservation. The early Christians employed it was well: think of the many vivid images and the absence of names — especially of wicked emperors — in the book of Revelation.

Some 1,200 years later, Dante broke the mold in *The Divine Comedy,* in which he fearlessly catalogued historic figures he considered to be wicked. Dante put several people in hell who were still alive on earth or who had only just recently died: Fra Alberigo and Branca d'Oria (Canto 33), and even Pope Boniface VIII (Canto 19). Dante ran great risks by placing contemporaries and near-contemporaries in hell, but he'd already been sent into exile and felt that telling the truth as he saw it was the most important thing.

And the Essenes' caution may have been all for naught anyway — their end came not through the "Lion of Wrath" or the "Wicked Priest," but through the Romans, the very group that they felt most confident of vanquishing!

Would it be more accurate to call the Essenes ascetics or apocalypticists?

You could call them both — depending on your definition of "asceticism." An ascetic is someone who practices strict self-denial, usually for spiritual reasons, and the Essenes certainly fit this description. They led strictly moral lives, and Josephus said some of them were celibate (see page 88). Yet all of this was for apocalyptic purposes: in order to prepare the way of the Lord, they disciplined themselves according to the rules of ancient warfare, purifying themselves before God. Only through strict restraint would they be ready to fight the final battle.

We might call their approach "apocalyptic asceticism," rejecting an indulgent, materialistic way of life because the kingdom of God was due at any moment. The Essenes made their exodus into the desert and waited for the three messianic figures to lead them into battle and rid the world of evil. They saw themselves as the New Israel born into the New Covenant in the last days. And they strove to walk perfectly in all God's ways, as ascetics and apocalypticists.

Was Jesus more or less apocalyptically-minded than the people of Qumrân?

If an apocalyptical mindset means having surreal visions, computing dates, applying Scripture to contemporary events, and calling the present the "end times," then I think Jesus and the Essenes were equally eschatological. The thing is, it's hard to find anybody in Judea in the first century A.D. who *wasn't* apocalyptically-minded, apart from the Herodians, who had their king and were in favor of the status quo.

Particularly when political conditions are oppressive or when a previously stable social order begins rapidly to change, pious people tend to imagine that the end is close at hand. With the Roman occupation and the advance of Hellenistic culture, both those conditions were met in first-century Judea. The times were extraordinary and it would have been very hard not to see them as a prelude to the consummation of history, even though, in the end, history just kept on going.

What's Next?

Millar Burrows, another Scrolls scholar, once said, "Perhaps the best thing the Dead Sea Scrolls can do for us is to make us appreciate our Bible all the more by contrast." Do you think the Dead Sea Scrolls play this role? Are they self-effacing, pointing beyond themselves to the Hebrew Bible?

Not really. I'm not interested in that line of thinking. I think we can value the Dead Sea Scrolls in their own right and not worry about making comparisons to the Bible or any other sacred texts. The Dead Sea Scrolls stand alone as invaluable remnants of a unique, ancient Jewish community. The sectarian documents — The War Scroll, the Damascus Document, and so forth — may not rise to canonical status, but that's a result of the actions of religious leaders and the circumstances surrounding councils.

The Essenes were extremely devoted and their reasoning powers were very strong. They created a whole world out of their traditions, both in writing and in practice, which is an admirable accomplishment.

If a remnant of the Essenes still exists today, where would we find it? Would its members be hermits in desert caves?

It's an interesting question. There must be over 100 sectarian, utopian movements in the United States alone, although none that I know of inhabit caves! Some do inhabit remote areas in the desert; the most striking example is the Mormon fundamentalist community that dominates two small towns on the border between Utah and Arizona. These communities still practice polygamy and, in some cases, child marriage, although they manage to conceal most of it from the authorities, who intervene only when a really flagrant case attracts national attention.

Elsewhere around the world, other sectarian groups might take specific passages of Scripture very seriously, while sharing a doctrinal foundation with mainstream believers. They might continue to live where they always have, and just form a new church to worship God as they see fit.

One thing about all these communities, wherever they're located and whenever they've existed throughout history, is that they are almost all concerned with restoring the purity of another age. The idea is that mainstream society, or the mainstream church, is just too far gone to save, so they isolate themselves.

What can contemporary communities learn from the experiences of the Qumrân sect?

For most of us, the biggest lesson from Qumrân is that you can not only *survive*, but *thrive* under arduous conditions. As far as we can tell, the Qumrân community was successful, and that took the efforts of a cooperative, determined group. What did they have to work with? Almost nothing. The estimates of the population are never more than a few hundred.

The Essenes were very literate, smart, and fully aware that in order to survive, they needed to work together according to rigorous rules. Working together, they designed a complicated water system, maintained a large library of at least 800 manuscripts, and held large community meals.

After surrendering all of his possessions, an initiate was completely dependent upon the group, and he was guaranteed survival. The Essenes had to be careful about every aspect of their survival, which is a practical reason for why the rules were so stringent — basically to adapt people to a very rigorous life. They traded personal freedom for a share in a common enterprise that provided a purposeful life and a share in a glorious future.

Now that we know the dates of the Scrolls and have published translations of all of them, what are Dead Sea Scrolls scholars going to do with their time?

I think the book is really closed on the Dead Sea Scrolls. There is not a whole lot more to learn. We just have to fill in a few gaps in the overall picture. After that, we can only wait for the next big discovery — which would call for more study and more publications.

By contrast, the work on the Hebrew Bible is endless: always more work, more analysis, more interpretation, more publication. The Bible remains a great challenge.

Would practicing some of the Essenes' rituals improve the spiritual life of any religious person, whether Jewish, Muslim, Christian, Buddhist, or Hindu?

Life is a matter of the spirit. A little variety in religious practice is interesting and entertaining. Respectful dialogue between religious traditions always leads to more peace. And the Essenes were a ritually pure, devout group who really lived and died as martyrs. In other words, their faith was their reason to live and die. Some people talk about restoring the Qumrân community and living at the recolonized site.

My sense is that the story of the original Qumrân settlement would make a great movie. The question is — who's going to write the script?

A Dead Sea Scrolls Glossary

Whether you're reading a book about the Dead Sea Scrolls, or visiting a Scrolls exhibition at a museum, you're bound to run into some words, names, and terms that are unfamiliar. This glossary is meant to be a guide to that scholarly language.

Albright, W. F. A seminal twentieth-century biblical scholar, a preeminent Dead Sea Scrolls scholar, archaeologist, and paleographer. Albright (1891-1971) directed the American School of Oriental Research in Jerusalem for 12 years (1920-29, 1933-36) and served as the W. W. Spence Professor of Semitic Languages in the Oriental Seminary of The Johns Hopkins University, Baltimore, Maryland, where he mentored David Noel Freedman, this book's co-author. Albright wrote numerous seminal works in the field, including *From the Stone Age to Christianity* (1940-46), *Archeology and the Religion of Israel* (1942-46), and *The Bible and the Ancient Near East* (1961). It is not an exaggeration to say that Albright influenced most biblical scholarship of the twentieth century. See also Higher Criticism.

Aleppo Codex Without question, the best text we have of the Hebrew Bible dating to the ninth or early tenth century A.D., but large segments are missing, leaving less than two-thirds of the manuscript. As a codex or folio, not a scroll, pages are double-sided, so when one sheet is missing, it is equivalent to the loss of two pages of text. Dr. Umberto Cassuto, a prominent biblical scholar, examined the Codex in the synagogue of the Syrian port town of Aleppo and saw it as complete. Surprisingly, after Israel's War of Independence in 1947-48, the Codex was found damaged: the Torah was gone (Genesis, Exodus, Leviticus, Numbers, and most of Deuteronomy), along with numerous leaves in the body of the manuscript in several books at the end of the Writings. See also Leningrad Codex.

Antiochus IV   Ruler of the Hellenistic Seleucid Empire, including Judah, from 175-164 B.C.. When Mattathias the Hasmonean (one of the Maccabees) resisted his program of Hellenization, Antiochus IV relented, ceased his program of religious persecution, and no longer forbade loyalty to the Torah. He is the archenemy referred to in the latter chapters of the book of Daniel. Before the Maccabean rebellion, Antiochus IV established an altar to the god Ba'al at the Jewish Temple, thinking that he was honoring Yahweh, the God of Israel, by blending the names of Ba'al and Yahweh into "Ba'al, the Lord of Heaven" (see Daniel 11:31; 1 Maccabees 1:5). The biblical authors condemn the altar as "the abomination of desolation," the most condemnatory epithet attributed to any object in the Hebrew Bible.

Apocalypse   Literally means "revelation," and in the biblical sense it is related to events leading up to the end of the world as we know it. In the New Testament, the book of Revelation is also called the Apocalypse. See also Second Coming.

Apocrypha   Literally "hidden or obscure." Comparable to the sectarian documents found at Qumrân, the Apocrypha or Deuterocanonical books are 13 books included in the Septuagint and the Vulgate (the Latin Bible), but not in the original Hebrew Bible: 1 and 2 Esdras, Tobit, Judith, Additions to the Book of Esther, the Wisdom of Solomon, Ecclesiasticus, Baruch, the Epistle of Jeremiah, the Additions to the Book of Daniel, the Prayer of Manasseh, and 1-2 Maccabees. The term can also refer to similar works relating to the New Testament. Apocryphal books are not considered to be divinely inspired by Jews and Protestants and are therefore treated as supplements to the canonized books of the Hebrew Bible and New Testament. However, the Apocrypha were included in many Protestant Bibles until the late eighteenth century, and they are still part of the Roman Catholic and Eastern Orthodox Bibles. The Council of Trent (1548) and the First Vatican Council (1870) affirmed the canonical authority of these books.

Apostle Literally means "someone who is sent," as on a mission, which can apply to anyone but often refers to prophets in the Old Testament. In the Jewish community of the first century A.D., *saliah* is the Hebrew word for someone who is sent, for example, by the high priest in Jerusalem to deliver official communiqués of the Sanhedrin and to collect money from the Jewish communities throughout the Roman Empire. When St. Paul travels throughout the diaspora in the Roman Empire, he finds a Jewish population in every city in which he founds a church. He, too, brings word from Jerusalem (see Acts 15) and collects money for the saints. More technically, in the New Testament the word "apostle" is restricted to the twelve chosen by Jesus to be his followers. The number twelve was derived from the twelve sons of the patriarch Jacob, and the apostles are described as ruling in the messianic age to come, with one of the apostles sitting on each one of the twelve thrones and judging the twelve tribes of Israel (Matthew 19:28). The word is also used of others besides the twelve, including a woman, Phoebe, a helper of many; and Prisca (or Priscilla), whom St. Paul called his missionary co-worker and praised for risking her neck for him (Romans 16:1-4).

Aramaic   A northwest Semitic language, a cousin of biblical Hebrew. Parts of the Hebrew Bible are written in biblical Aramaic, one of many Aramaic dialects. Aramaic was the common language of the Persian Empire and more widespread than Hebrew, which was only spoken in two small nations, Israel and Judah. See also Semitic.

Bedouin   The plural form of the Arabic word *bedu,* a true nomad who does not settle anywhere. Some groups in antiquity are described by Dr. W. F. Albright of Johns Hopkins University as "seminomadic" because they move back and forth between designated locations following the agricultural season. Some plant crops in the spring and return in the fall for harvest, but they are somewhere between nomadic and settled. In our day, even the Bedouin are settling down, which suggests that the anthropological process transitioning from nomad to seminomad to settlers seems to be continuous. See also Albright, W. F.

Canon   Literally, a "reed" that was used as a measuring stick. In its literary sense, a canon is the exclusive list of authoritative books that are considered to be the sacred word of God, written by and about inspired people, beginning with Moses who is traditionally credited with being the author of the Torah or Pentateuch. The establishment of a canon is the final stage of a long, complex process of reflection and evaluation, beginning with a book's publication and official sanction within a community (see 2 Kings 23). Beginning in the sixth century B.C. during the Babylonian Exile, the narrative called the Primary History (the Torah or Pentateuch followed by the former prophets making a continuous narrative, Genesis through Deuteronomy, and Joshua through Kings) was completed along with the related literature of the Latter Prophets and Writings to form the Hebrew Bible as we know it. The process was concluded in the time of Ezra and Nehemiah, around 420 B.C., with the exception of the book of Daniel, which was added in the second century B.C. By the time Ezra the scribe returned from Babylon in the mid-fifth century B.C. "with the Law of his God in his hand" (Ezra 7:14), most of the canon had already been circulating in its present form. Rabbis defined the Hebrew Bible at the so-called Council of Jamnia in A.D. 92, when the text was fixed. See also Apocrypha.

Children of Darkness   The Essenes' term for Maccabean Jews and Gentiles. The War Scroll, found among the Dead Sea Scrolls, is the classic apocalyptic document that divides everything into two classes: good and evil. The evil people are called the Children of Darkness (or Sons of Darkness) and are portrayed with relish in various places as being covetous, slack, deceitful, proud, cruel, hypocritical, impatient, frivolous, envious, lustful, and blasphemous, and as having blind eyes, deaf ears, stiff necks, and heavy hearts. The Essenes — joining forces with God and the angels Michael, Raphael, and Sariel — would defeat the Children of Darkness — led by the demon Belial — in the final, 40-year battle. See also Children of Light.

Children of Light   The Essenes' term for themselves. The War Scroll paints the righteous Children of Light (or Sons of Light) as God-fearing, humble, merciful, good, intelligent, wise, zealous, holy, affectionate, pure, and modest. They are promised a long, healthy, and happy life: "As for the visitation of all who walk by it, it will be healing, abundant peace, length of days, fruitfulness of seed, together with everlasting blessing and eternal joy in life without end, a crown of glory, and a garment of honor in everlasting light." See also Children of Darkness.

Conventicle   A community or commune such as the one at Qumrân. The term also described similar groups that lived in cities.

Copper Scroll   A sectarian document found at Qumrân in the form of a copper plaque rolled to look like two scrolls. It lists 64 locations where treasure, allegedly from King Solomon's temple, is supposedly buried around the Dead Sea region.

Damascus Document   The supplemental rulebook, a sectarian scroll found at Qumrân. Part One exhorts the community to meditate on the lessons of Israel's history to avoid the fate of the wicked apostates, and Part Two is a Constitution that regulates membership.

Dead Sea Scrolls   Hailed as "the greatest archaeological discovery of the twentieth century," the Dead Sea Scrolls were found by two Bedouin shepherd boys in the Dead Sea region of Palestine in 1947. Originally the property of a monastic group known as the Essenes, the Scrolls — fragments of papyrus, leather, and, in one case, copper — represent 39 books from the Hebrew Bible and the so-called Apocrypha that were once part of complete books in scroll form. However, when scholars refer to the "Dead Sea Scrolls," they often mean the non-biblical, sectarian documents such as the Manual of Discipline or the Damascus Document found at Qumrân.

Deuterocanonical   The official designation given to the apocryphal books by the Catholic and Orthodox churches. See Apocrypha.

Diaspora   The Jews scattered beyond the Holy Land in many Greek and Roman cities and elsewhere in the Hellenistic Age. The Jewish dispersion began after the kingdom of Israel was conquered in 722 B.C., Judah fell to the Babylonians in 597 B.C., and Jerusalem was destroyed in 586 B.C. Jews either migrated or were taken into exile, both of which constitute the diaspora. The first-century historian Flavius Josephus estimates that there were several million Jews in the diaspora in the first century, which may be an exaggeration. We know there was a large Jewish population not only in Jerusalem, but also in Alexandria and Rome. And in practically every city he visits, St. Paul finds fellow Jews. See also Exodus.

Documentary Hypothesis   A hypothesis about the composition of the first six books of the Bible, brought to its classic form by Dr. Julius Wellhausen (1844-1918), a professor at the University of Göttingen in Germany and proponent of Higher Criticism. While the theory was commonly accepted among German scholars at the time, Wellhausen is credited with the classic statement of the Documentary Hypothesis, which explains the composition of the Hexateuch: the Torah, or Pentateuch (Genesis, Exodus, Leviticus, Numbers, Deuteronomy), plus the book of Joshua. The Documentary Hypothesis explains that four manuscript tradition, or sources, were used in compiling the Hexateuch. A letter designates each manuscript tradition: J (Jahwist or Yahwist), E (Elohist), D (Deuteronomist), and P (Priestly). Because some of the material used in these six biblical books is reflective of concerns from a later period during Israel's monarchy, the hypothesis revolutionized biblical scholarship. See also Higher Criticism.

Emend   To change or correct a manuscript, which should be a last resort for an editor. One kind of non-obtrusive emendation is simply comparing manuscripts and picking the best reading. "Conjectural emendation" is a more invasive method of emending a text; it happens when an editor is convinced there is something wrong with the text and changes one or more words without any manuscript evidence to support such a change, usually based on prior understanding and interests.

Eschatology   The study of last things. In a religious context, eschatology is the notion that the world will come to an end suddenly and violently. Books like Daniel in the Old Testament or Revelation in the New Testament provide dramatic clues and depictions of the end. These concerns flourish during times of great crisis, when the persecuted believers urgently pray for the intervention of God and an end to their trials and tribulations when God comes to settle scores and punish the evildoers, while saving the innocent and faithful. See also Apocalypse.

Essene   A member of a Jewish sect that existed between the second century B.C. and the second century A.D. The origin of the word is uncertain, but may be the Aramaic form of *Hasidim,* "pious ones." Josephus, the Jewish historian, calls them *Essēnoi* or *Essaioi,* which is most likely the Greek corruption of the Hebrew *'ôśê hattôrāh* ("doers of the Law"). The community at Qumrân is widely believed to have been made up of Essenes. See also Dead Sea Scrolls, Children of Light.

Exegesis   Literally "to guide or lead out," as in bringing out what a text means and studying every aspect of its language, content, and historical context.

Exodus   Literally "going out," from *ex-* (out) and *-hodos* (way). In the Hebrew Bible, this is the basic national experience and tradition of leaving slavery in Egypt for a new Eden, a Land of Promise: Canaan (present-day Israel, the West Bank, and Syria). The postexilic picture is the Second Exodus out of exile in Babylon. "Exodus" has become symbolic of much else: any departure from a presently intolerable or undesirable environment into a better place. The language of the Exodus is appropriated for leaving the place of imprisonment and suffering and entering a whole new world.

Fundamentalism   Broadly speaking, a belief in strict conformity to literal readings of sacred texts. See Sect.

Genesis Apocryphon   A document found among the Dead Sea Scrolls that embellishes the stories found in the biblical book of Genesis.

Hasidim   From the Hebrew *Hasid.* Literally "pious ones" who are faithful and orthodox, with a heroic tradition of not bowing to persecution. Scholars think that the Hasidim of the book of Daniel are the parent group from whom both Essenes and Pharisees emerge. See also Pharisees, Essenes.

Hellenism   Literally "the Greek way of life," a summation of Greek religious and cultural identity. For many Jews, Hellenism was antithetical to "the Hebrew way of life." Hellenism introduced Greek language and cultural institutions, the philosophy of Plato and Aristotle, theater, sculpture, gymnasiums, temples, and architecture, all of which literally changed the face of the earth. The Hellenistic Age lasted for three centuries after Alexander the Great's reign, when Rome conquered the whole eastern world. Today, the western world is admittedly more Hellenistic than Judaic, and that was true for many Jews in the first century as well. Today, western religion is predominantly Judeo-Christian, replacing the Greco-Roman pantheon, but we are heirs of Greek philosophy and science.

Higher Criticism   A method of Bible study by which, applying scientific principles and historical methods to the Bible, German biblical scholars of the eighteenth and nineteenth centuries sought to avoid subjective, confessional, or theological interpretations. Instead, they mainly relied upon internal evidence to determine and authenticate the chronological order of various texts, as well as the author's identity and purpose for writing. The founder of the theoretical school was the

French scholar Jean Astruc, a Pentateuch scholar in the mid-eighteenth century. Higher criticism was attacked for discrediting Christianity and ignoring its spiritual dimensions, and the practice has largely been abandoned for other methodologies, such as narrative criticism (the study of how stories are made) and canonical criticism (retracing how texts became accepted as Scripture). See also Documentary Hypothesis.

J, E, D, P (or J, E, P, D)   See Documentary Hypothesis.

Josephus, Flavius   An indispensable historian as one of the few authors outside of the New Testament to write about contemporary events in the first century A.D. He was a general in the Jewish army during the war against Rome (A.D. 66-73) who surrendered early to the Romans, was pardoned, moved to Rome, and became a favorite of the Emperor Vespasian. With a sizable pension from the State in the Augustan Age, and as a renaissance man of letters, he wrote the seven-volume *Jewish War* and the twenty-volume *Jewish Antiquities,* covering the history of the Jews from creation in Genesis through the whole history of the Jewish people to the final catastrophic revolt against Roman authority. As a man educated in the classics (including the poetry of Horace and Virgil) and fluent in Aramaic and in Greek, his writings are sophisticated, masterful, and the only available sources for much of this important history from someone who lived through the events. He was not only an eyewitness and participant in much of this story, but also a shrewd observer and accurate reporter.

Judah (or Judea)   The southern kingdom after Israel divided, lasting from David's reign in 1000 B.C. until the Babylonian exile in 587/586 B.C. Judah's monarchy consisted of a single dynasty in the line of David, the first king of Judah and the successor of Saul, and then his son, Solomon, renowned for wisdom and for building the first Temple.

Leningrad Codex The oldest, most complete manuscript of the Hebrew Bible, dating from A.D. 1008, approximately 1,000 years after the Dead Sea Scrolls, and based on the Masoretic Text of the Hebrew Bible. See also Aleppo Codex, Masoretic Text.

Levite Members of the tribe of Levi. The tribe of Levi didn't receive a territorial allotment in the land of Canaan. Instead, Levites were assigned 48 cities throughout the tribal regions, enabling them to settle in both kingdoms: Israel in the north, and Judah in the south. In the Temple, two groups of Levites were in attendance: (1) priests, directly descended from Aaron, the first high priest and the brother of Moses; and (2) all other Levites, who served in various capacities (somewhat like deacons and altar boys or acolytes). The prophet Ezekiel further restricts the priesthood and entrusts the most sacred things not just to Levites, but only to Zadokites within that tribe. See also Zadokite.

Lion of Wrath The sobriquet used in the Dead Sea Scrolls most likely for the Sadducee Alexander Jannaeus, the belligerent priest-king of Judea from 103-76 B.C. who opposed the Pharisees. In the Talmud — the rabbinic book of commentary on the law — Alexander Jannaeus appears as the wicked tyrant, "King Yannai." See also Talmud.

Liturgy In Judaism, the formal service in the Tabernacle or Temple, and in later synagogues, the specific rites, observances, and procedures with a fixed set of prayers and pronouncements. The sectarian documents found among the Dead Sea Scrolls are preoccupied with liturgy, placing a premium on all practices that fostered ritual cleanliness.

Maccabees The priestly family that ruled the Jews from 160 to 63 B.C. — when the Romans entered Jerusalem. The Maccabees liberated Israel from Syrian oppression in the 160s B.C. Mattathias, the first Maccabean ruler, reigned first as king and then as both king and high priest, followed in turn by his sons Judas, Jonathan, and Simon. The decades of the Maccabean Wars against the Seleucid rulers, which are narrated in 1 and 2 Maccabees in the Apocrypha and are also referred to in Daniel, were defined by a struggle between religious Jews like the Maccabees and secularizing Hellenizers. See also Hellenism.

Manual of Discipline   One of the Dead Sea Scrolls. The Manual of Discipline explains the community's purpose, initiation rites, theology, and penal codes. It was the Qumranites' guidebook for the *maśkîl,* or master instructor, whose job was "to instruct and teach all the Sons of Light about the generations of all humanity, each according to the kinds of spirits they possess and their deeds in their lifetime."

Masoretic Text   A widely used text of the Hebrew Bible. The name refers to the *masorah:* vowel signs, accents, and marginal notes added to the consonantal Hebrew text by scribes in A.D. 600-950 in order to preserve accurate transmission, reading, and copying of the text. See also Aleppo Codex and Leningrad Codex.

Messiah   Literally "the anointed one." In the Hebrew Bible, it is not used in an eschatological, apocalyptic sense. Three categories of people could be anointed, usually with oil: kings, priests, and prophets (the prophets only in principle but not in practice; at least we have no examples). Eventually the term came to refer to the future Messiah, the savior who would appear at the end times (and who Christians believe came in the person of Jesus).

Paleography   Literally "old writing," which could be on scrolls, stones, metal, or any other surface. Usually used to mean the study of such writing.

Paleo-Hebrew   The earliest form of the Hebrew language. Paleo-Hebrew was considered a sacred script by the Essenes. See also Semitic.

Pentateuch   Literally "five books." The term refers to the first five books of the Hebrew Bible, traditionally thought to have been authored by Moses: Genesis, Exodus, Leviticus, and Deuteronomy. See also Torah.

Pesharim   Sectarian scrolls found at Qumrân. The *pesharim* interpret passages from the Psalms and the Prophets, finding hidden meanings that make the text directly relevant to the historical and social situation of the Qumrân community. The best known is the *Pesher* or Commentary on Habakkuk, one of the seven Scrolls discovered in Cave 1. The author of this *pesher* found a reference in Habakkuk to a real-life confrontation between the so-called Wicked Priest and the community's Teacher of Righteousness, an event that was vividly etched into the community's memory.

Pharisee   From the root *paras,* meaning "to divide or separate." With the Sadducees, Essenes, and Zealots, the Pharisees were one of the four traditional first-century Jewish groups listed by the historian Josephus. The Pharisees were the branch of Judaism that was more meticulous about defining and describing religion, which they took very seriously. The Pharisees were the active stimulus for religious observance, and because the rabbis emerged from this branch of Judaism, they defined the future of Judaism. They come to life in the New Testament, but that is also where they receive a lot of bad press. We should recognize that the New Testament gives the Pharisees attention because they played an important role in Jewish society, and although they opposed Jesus at times, they were also his colleagues who had challenging and productive creative exchanges with him. See also Sadducee, Essene.

Ptolemy I   Ptolemy I (reigned 305-282 B.C.) was Alexander the Great's general, who founded the enduring Ptolemaic Dynasty in Egypt. After Alexander's death, he successfully outmaneuvered Alexander's other three generals to retain Egypt as his territory. He often warred with Seleucus, the general who ruled from Syria to Afghanistan, and was able to seize parts of Syria and Palestine. Centuries later, after Ptolemy XII died, his daughter, Cleopatra VII (reigned from 51-30 B.C.) jointly ruled with her younger brother Ptolemy XIV (47-44 B.C.) until she had him assassinated. Cleopatra's son Ptolemy XV (36-30 B.C.), allegedly the son of Julius Caesar, was the final dynastic ruler. See also Seleucid.

Qumrân   The Essenes' settlement near a series of caves by the Dead Sea. Its history can be summarized as follows: it began around 125 B.C., was destroyed by an earthquake in 31 B.C., was rebuilt in 5 B.C., and was destroyed by the Tenth Roman Legion in A.D. 68. See also Essene.

Sadducee   A traditional, more conservative branch of Judaism that preferred tradition above change. Sadducees were connected with the priesthood and associated with the wealthy, ruling class. See also Pharisee.

Sect   A religious group that parts from the majority on particular aspects of doctrine and practice, focusing on those differences. See also Fundamentalism.

Seleucid   Dynasty founded by Seleucus, one of Alexander the Great's four generals who divided and ruled Alexander's empire after his death, and after contesting the territories for 40 years with the three other generals. Seleucid territory stretched from Syria to Afghanistan, including Judah. Seleucus was perpetually warring with Ptolemy I, Alexander's former general who ruled in Egypt. After 150 years, the Seleucids' decentralized rule weakened their control to such an extent that by the time of the Roman conquest, the Seleucid Empire was confined to a small part of northern Syria. See also Ptolemy I.

Semitic A language group that includes Hebrew, and also the culture that it represents. The name comes from Shem, one of the three sons of Noah. See Paleo-Hebrew.

Septuagint (LXX) Literally *septuaginta,* which is the Greek for 70 (LXX), which is the abbreviated, round number of scribes — officially 72 — who translated the Hebrew Bible into Greek. The tradition is that 70 elders were locked in separate cells, and each wrote a translation that was identical to the others. While the story is legendary, the premise is that a substantial group of Jewish scholars undertook the task of translating the Hebrew Bible into Greek sometime in the third century B.C. Their work continued for another hundred years or more until all of the books were translated into Greek.

Talmud Literally "the study." Rabbinic Judaism's great store of knowledge, second only to the Hebrew Bible, that sets Judaism apart from other faith traditions that claim their origins in the Hebrew Bible. The Talmud is the multi-volume collection of oral traditions recorded in two works: the Mishnah and the Gemarah. The Mishnah is written in Hebrew and codifies the law. The Gemarah is written in the Aramaic vernacular and is much longer than the Mishnah — expansive in its presentation of the dialectical thought processes in debates about the Hebrew Bible in academies of Babylon in the third through the sixth centuries A.D. Two traditions have produced a Talmud: the more commonly-used Babylonian Talmud, and the less authoritative and shorter Palestinian Talmud. See also Torah.

Teacher of Righteousness The leader of the Essenes at Qumrân. He was most likely a priest, and possibly a relative of the high priest in Jerusalem, Onias (Hananiah III). Most likely he ruled the community jointly with a secular leader, the *paqîd,* or supervisor or overseer. He was seen as a precursor to the messianic prophet, priest, and king the Essenes expected to come. See also Wicked Priest and Zadokite.

Temple Scroll   One of the Dead Sea Scrolls. The Temple Scroll contains the Essenes' own, stricter version of Jewish ritual law. Extensive but fragmentary, it was found by Bedouin in Cave 11.

Tetragrammaton   Literally "four letters" of God's name: YHWH. Used because of the uncertainty concerning which vowels to use in the pronunciation of the name, since Hebrew was originally written without vowels and they did not want to mispronounce — or even pronounce — the name of God due to its holiness. When the Masoretes added vowel points, they were assimilated from the Hebrew word *Adonay,* "my Lord."

Thanksgiving Psalms   A collection found among the Dead Sea Scrolls — partially intact — with other sectarian (noncanonical) books. The Thanksgiving Psalms form a prayer book of songs and hymns that acknowledge human sinfulness and praise their righteous God for delivering the community from tribulation. Many of these hymns begin with "I thank you, O Lord," which gives the Scroll its name.

Torah   Literally "law" or "instruction." The Torah, or Pentateuch, is comprised of the five "books of Moses" that are of the highest authority within the Hebrew Bible: Genesis, Exodus, Leviticus, Numbers, and Deuteronomy. The Torah binds the people to a divine covenant and obliges them to obey rules and laws. Other parts of the Hebrew Bible (the Prophets and Writings) are also very important — to be believed and followed — but they explain and instruct without binding people to terms of a contract, and therefore, do not carry the same weight of authority as the Torah. See also Talmud.

War Scroll The commonly-used name for one of the almost completely intact sectarian (non-canonical) Dead Sea Scrolls formally called "The Order of the War Between the Children of Light and the Children of Darkness." The War Scroll contains instructions for the final battle of history between the "Sons of Light" (the people of Qumrân) and the "Sons of Darkness" (profane Maccabean Jews and Gentiles) at the end of time. The War Scroll gives army formations and battle plans, lists the necessary military equipment, and gives specific prayers and battle cries for the high priest, who acts as the commander-in-chief in the absence of a messianic king. After a thanksgiving ceremony, a great and final battle ends history. The War Scroll describes the bloody aftermath, and the certain defeat of the Children of Darkness, with zeal. See also Children of Darkness, Children of Light.

Wellhausen, Julius See Documentary Hypothesis.

Wicked Priest Once a legitimate high priest, probably one of the Maccabees, who became corrupted in the eyes of the Essenes. See Teacher of Righteousness and Zadokite.

YHWH See Tetragrammaton.

Zadokite The only line of priests recognized by the Essenes as legitimate, in contrast to what the Essenes considered the "illegitimate" Maccabean line in charge of the Temple in their day. The name comes from Zadok, high priest during the reign of David and Solomon. The last truly Zadokite high priest was Hananiah III (Onias in Greek) who reigned from 196-175 B.C. All the high priests after him, although they were in the priestly group as sons of Aaron, lacked the Zadokite descent. See also Teacher of Righteousness and Wicked Priest.

David Noel Freedman's Select Bibliography on the Dead Sea Scrolls

If reading this book has made you want to learn more about the Dead Sea Scrolls, the Essenes, and Qumrân, the following titles, available at your local library or bookstore, will offer plenty of places to start digging more deeply.

Books and Articles Written or Co-Written by David Noel Freedman

Freedman, David Noel. "The Massoretic Text and the Qumran Scrolls: A Study in Orthography." In *Qumran and the History of the Biblical Text,* ed. Frank M. Cross and Shemaryahu Talmon, 196-211. Cambridge, Mass.: Harvard University Press, 1975; and in *Divine Commitment and Human Obligation: Selected Writings of David Noel Freedman,* vol. 2:13-28. Grand Rapids: Wm. B. Eerdmans, 1997.

————. "The Old Testament at Qumran." In *New Directions in Biblical Archaeology,* ed. David Noel Freedman and Jonas C. Greenfield, 117-26. Garden City: Doubleday, 1969.

————. "Prophecy in the Dead Sea Scrolls." In *The Dead Sea Scrolls and Christian Faith: In Celebration of the Jubilee Year of the Discovery of Qumran Cave 1,* ed. James H. Charlesworth and Walter P. Weaver, 42-57. Harrisburg: Trinity Press International, 1998.

———, Frank Moore Cross, and James M. Sanders. *Scrolls from Qumrân Cave 1: The Great Isaiah Scroll, The Order of the Community, The* Pesher *to Habakkuk.* Jerusalem: Albright Institute for Archaeological Research and The Shrine of the Book, 1972.

———, and Jeffrey C. Geoghegan. "Another Stab at the Wicked Priest." In *The Bible and the Dead Sea Scrolls,* vol. 2, ed. J. H. Charlesworth. North Richland Hills, BIBAL, 2000.

———, and Kenneth A. Mathews. *The Paleo-Hebrew Leviticus Scroll (11QpaleoLev).* Winona Lake: Eisenbrauns, 1985.

———, and Leona Glidden Running. *William Foxwell Albright: A Twentieth Century Genius.* New York: Two Continents, 1975.

———, and Laura Zucconi. "Who Was Who and What Was What Among the Qumran Sectarians." *Festschrift in Honor of Fred Young.* In Press.

Books Edited by David Noel Freedman

Allegro, John M. *The People of the Dead Sea Scrolls.* Garden City: Doubleday, 1958.

———. *The Treasure of the Copper Scroll.* Garden City: Doubleday, 1960.

Charlesworth, James H. *Jesus and the Dead Sea Scrolls.* New York: Doubleday, 1992.

Collins, John J. *The Scepter and the Star: The Messiahs of the Dead Sea Scrolls and Other Ancient Literature.* New York: Doubleday, 1995; rev. ed., Grand Rapids: Wm. B. Eerdmans, forthcoming.

Schiffman, Lawrence H. *Reclaiming the Dead Sea Scrolls: The History of Judaism, the Background of Christianity, the Lost Library of Qumran.* Philadelphia: Jewish Publication Society, 1994.

Other Recommended Titles

Abegg, Martin G., Jr., Peter Flint, and Eugene C. Ulrich. *The Dead Sea Scrolls Bible: The Oldest Known Bible.* San Francisco: HarperSanFrancisco, 1999.

Allegro, John M. *The Dead Sea Scrolls and the Christian Myth.* 2nd ed. Buffalo: Prometheus, 1992.

Benoit, Pierre. *Paul and the Dead Sea Scrolls,* ed. Jerome Murphy-O'Connor and James H. Charlesworth. New York: Crossroad, 1990.

Brown, Judith Anne. *John Marco Allegro: The Maverick of the Dead Sea Scrolls.* Grand Rapids: Wm. B. Eerdmans, 2005.

Brown, Raymond E. *John and the Dead Sea Scrolls,* ed. James H. Charlesworth. New York: Crossroad, 1990.

Burrows, Millar. *The Dead Sea Scrolls.* New York: Viking, 1955.

—————. *More Light on the Dead Sea Scrolls: New Scrolls and New Interpretations.* New York: Viking, 1958.

Cross, Frank Moore. *The Ancient Library of Qumran.* 3rd ed. Minneapolis: Fortress, 1995.

Fitzmyer, Joseph A. *Responses to 101 Questions on the Dead Sea Scrolls.* New York: Paulist, 1992.

Friedman, Richard Elliott. *Who Wrote the Bible?* 2nd ed. San Francisco: HarperSanFrancisco, 1997.

Trever, John C. *The Dead Sea Scrolls: A Personal Account.* Grand Rapids: Wm. B. Eerdmans, 1977.

VanderKam, James C. *The Dead Sea Scrolls Today.* Grand Rapids: Wm. B. Eerdmans, 1994.

—————, and Peter Flint. *The Meaning of the Dead Sea Scrolls: Their Significance for Understanding the Bible, Judaism, Jesus, and Christianity.* San Francisco: HarperSanFrancisco, 2002.